GUNNERS LISTS

GUNNERS
LISTS

250 lists of essential and
non-essential Arsenal facts

Chas Newkey-Burden

hamlyn

An Hachette UK Company
www.hachette.co.uk

First published in Great Britain in 2009 by
Hamlyn, a division of Octopus Publishing Group Ltd
2–4 Heron Quays, London E14 4JP
www.octopusbooks.co.uk

ISBN 978-0-600-61875-1

A CIP catalogue record for this book is available from the British Library

Printed and bound in China

10 9 8 7 6 5 4 3 2 1

CONTENTS

Ages of man *41*

The fairer sex *46*

Scoring, scoring Arsenal *49*

Cool Britannia *254*

Extra time *261*

INTRODUCTION

For as long as men have kicked balls round muddy fields, those watching them have catalogued what they've witnessed into lists. Accordingly, the humble list has become almost as much a part of the beautiful game as the boot, the net and the referee's whistle. It's not hard to work out why. Football has always attracted those hungry for stats, facts and opinions. Mix those three ingredients together and the end result is the list.

However ravenous your appetite for the list is, this book will satisfy it. With 250 Top 10s about your favourite football club, it gives you 2,500 facts to feast on. It covers the essential, the obscure and everything in between. You can find out the Top 10 appearances-makers, Top 10 ginger Gunners and the 10 most common first names of players in the Club's history. The scope is huge. As you flick through these pages you will not just be informed, you will also be reminded of great moments in your own supporting life including the highest wins over Tottenham Hotspur, the most delightful debuts and the top victories in the Champions League.

These pages include some illustrious 'guest lists' thanks to the Arsenal legends who have contributed their own Top 10s. Bob Wilson names his 10 memories of the 1970–71 Double-winning campaign, Steve Bould reveals his Top 10 defensive giants and former Club captain Kenny Sansom lists his favourite 10 Gunners players. Dennis Bergkamp, one of the beautiful game's most poetic and celebrated number 10s, chips in with a finely crafted Top 10 of his own. Famous fans, too, have added their own lists and included in this section are contributions from comedians Paul Kaye and Hardeep Singh Kohli, actor and broadcaster Tom Watt, musician Shovell and BBC *Breakfast News* presenter Chris Hollins (son of former Arsenal captain John Hollins).

Compiling this book was an extensive task aided by numerous sources. These included the official Club website www.arsenal.com and other sites rich in football facts, stats and trivia including: www.soccerbase.com, www.thefa.com, www.uefa.com, www.bbc.co.uk and stats.football365.com. Numerous books were consulted including *The Official Arsenal Factfile*, *The Official Illustrated History Of Arsenal*, *Arsenal Stadium History*, *The Official Arsenal Encyclopedia*, *Arsenal Player By Player*, *The Official Arsenal Miscellany*, *The All-New Official Arsenal Miscellany* and *Arsenal Premiership Player Profiles*.

A pile of matchday programmes and editions of the official *Arsenal Magazine* big enough to cover the pitch at the Emirates Stadium were also consulted. Just as indispensable were the numerous Club employees, Arsenal fans and other friends – see the Acknowledgements page for the full list – who pointed me in the right direction during the painstaking, gargantuan search for facts and stats. Unless otherwise specified in a list, the word 'appearances' refers to appearances (including as a substitute) in League, FA Cup, League Cup and European matches.

Important statistics, bizarre facts and mind-bending trivia: this book will inform, amuse and surprise you again and again. From the Top 10 Arsenal animals to the 10 most memorable hairstyles and the 10 tallest Gunners, this feast of weird and wonderful facts is essential reading for all Arsenal fans. After all, why settle for just one 'perfect 10' when you can have 250 of them?

TOP 10 OVERALL
APPEARANCE-MAKERS

	Player	Games
1	David O'Leary	719
2	Tony Adams	665
3	George Armstrong	621
4	Lee Dixon	614
5	Nigel Winterburn	579
6	David Seaman	560
7	Pat Rice	527
8	Peter Storey	501
9	John Radford	481
10	Peter Simpson	477

David O'Leary made his debut against Burnley on 16/8/1975 and his final appearance as a substitute in the victorious FA Cup Final against Sheffield Wednesday on 20/5/1993. His fellow substitute that evening, Ian Selley, was a 1-year-old when O'Leary played his first game for the Club.

TOP 10 APPEARANCE-MAKING GOALKEEPERS

	Player	Games
1	David Seaman	560
2	Jack Kelsey	351
3	Pat Jennings	326
4	Bob Wilson	308
5	John Lukic	297
6	George Swindin	294
7	Jens Lehmann	198
8	Jimmy Rimmer	146
9	Manuel Almunia	125
10	Alex Wilson	89

	Player	Games
1	David O'Leary	719
2	Tony Adams	665
3	Lee Dixon	614
4	Nigel Winterburn	579
5	Pat Rice	527
6	Peter Simpson	477
7	Bob John	467
8	Martin Keown	445
9	Eddie Hapgood	434
10	Kenny Sansom	394

TOP 10 APPEARANCE-MAKING MIDFIELDERS

	Player	Games
1	George Armstrong	621
2	Peter Storey	501
3	Graham Rix	463
4	Ray Parlour	462
5	Paul Davis	445
6	Paul Merson	422
7	Patrick Vieira	406
8	Frank McLintock	403
9	Brian Talbot	326
10	George Graham	308

TOP 10 APPEARANCE-MAKING STRIKERS

	Player	Games
1	John Radford	481
2	Dennis Bergkamp	423
3	Thierry Henry	380
4	Alan Smith	345
5	Billy Blyth	341
6	Jimmy Logie	326
7	Don Roper	319
8	Frank Stapleton	299
9	Ian Wright	287
10	Alan Sunderland	280

TOP 10 LEAGUE APPEARANCE-MAKERS AT HIGHBURY*

	Player	Games
1	Tony Adams	162
2	David O'Leary	256
3	George Armstrong	248
4	Lee Dixon	220
5	Nigel Winterburn	215
6	Bob John	214
7	David Seaman	202
8	Pat Rice	199
9	Eddie Hapgood	197
10	Peter Storey	190

* These figures do not include substitute appearances.

	Player	Games
1	Tony Adams	665
2	Pat Rice	527
3	Eddie Hapgood	434
4	Patrick Vieira	406
5	Frank McLintock	403
6	Kenny Sansom	394
7	Tom Parker	258
8	Joe Mercer	247
9=	Alex James	231
=	Cesc Fabregas	231

* These figures refer to the number of Arsenal appearances each captain made, not how many appearances they made wearing the captain's armband. Correct to the end of the 2008–09 season.

TOP 10 LEAGUE APPEARANCES IN THE 1988–89 SEASON*

	Player	Games
1=	John Lukic	38
=	David Rocastle	38
=	Nigel Winterburn	38
4=	Paul Merson	37
=	Michael Thomas	37
6=	Tony Adams	36
=	Alan Smith	36
8	Kevin Richardson	34
9	Lee Dixon	33
10	Brian Marwood	31

* Championship-winning season.

	Player	Games
1=	Steve Bould	38
=	Lee Dixon	38
=	David Seaman	38
=	Nigel Winterburn	38
5=	Paul Davis	37
=	Paul Merson	37
=	Alan Smith	37
8	Anders Limpar	34
9	Perry Groves	32
10	Michael Thomas	31

* Championship-winning season.

TOP 10 LEAGUE APPEARANCES IN THE 1997-98 SEASON*

	Player	Games
1	Nigel Winterburn	36
2	Ray Parlour	34
3	Patrick Vieira	33
4=	Marc Overmars	32
=	Emmanuel Petit	32
6=	David Platt	31
=	David Seaman	31
8=	Dennis Bergkamp	28
=	Lee Dixon	28
10=	Tony Adams	26
=	Nicolas Anelka	26

* Championship-winning season.

TOP 10 LEAGUE APPEARANCES IN THE 2001–02 SEASON*

	Player	Games
1	Patrick Vieira	36
2=	Dennis Bergkamp	33
=	Thierry Henry	33
=	Sylvain Wiltord	33
5	Sol Campbell	31
6	Ashley Cole	29
7	Robert Pires	28
8=	Lauren	27
=	Ray Parlour	27
10	Gilles Grimandi	26

* Championship-winning season.

TOP 10 LEAGUE APPEARANCES IN THE 2003–04 SEASON*

	Player	Games
1	Jens Lehmann	38
2	Thierry Henry	37
3	Robert Pires	36
4	Sol Campbell	35
5=	Ashley Cole	32
=	Gilberto	32
=	Lauren	32
8	Freddie Ljungberg	30
9	Patrick Vieira	29
10	Dennis Bergkamp	28

* Championship-winning season.

10 SINGLE-APPEARANCE
GUNNERS

	Player	Match	Date
1	Roy Goulden	v Leeds United (h)	24/2/1959
2	Roger Davidson	v Wolverhampton Wanderers (h)	16/3/1968
3	Jehad Muntasser	v Birmingham City (h)	14/10/1997
4	Isaiah Rankin	v Tottenham Hotspur (a)	28/10/1997
5	Julian Gray	v Newcastle United (a)	17/10/2000
6	Brian McGovern	v Newcastle United (a)	17/10/2000
7	Lee Canoville	v Ipswich Town (h)	1/11/2000
8	Rohan Rickets	v Manchester United (h)	5/11/2001
9	Carlin Itonga	v Manchester United (h)	5/11/2001
10	Michal Papadopulos	v Wolverhampton Wanderers (h)	2/12/2003

With the exception of Roy Goulden, all the players on this list made their one appearance as a substitute.

THE 10 LOWEST NUMBERS OF PLAYERS USED IN A SEASON*

	Nos.	Season
1	16	1968–69, 1970–71
2	17	1988–89
3	18	1984–85
4	19	1947–48, 1967–68, 1971–72, 1979–80, 1981–82, 1986–87, 1989–90, 1990–91
5	20	1948–49, 1956–57, 1973–74
6	21	1928–29, 1972–73
7	22	1949–50, 2003–04
8	24	1923–24, 1929–30, 1964–65
9	25	1934–35, 1936–37, 1995–96, 1998–99, 2006–07
10	26	1922–23, 1997–98

* These figures cover the 1919–20 season onwards, when reliable records began.

THE 10 HIGHEST HOME
ATTENDANCES

	Nos.	Match	Date
1	73,295	v Sunderland	9/3/1935
2	72,408	v Northampton Town	27/1/1951
3	72,164	v Tottenham Hotspur	29/9/1951
4	71,446	v Aston Villa	24/2/1926
5	69,466	v Barnsley	2/2/1952
6	69,158	v Blackpool	28/2/1953
7	69,051	v Tottenham Hotspur	7/2/1953
8	68,828	v Tottenham Hotspur	31/1/1934
9	67,445	v Derby County	18/2/1950
10	67,311	v Wolverhampton Wanderers	4/9/1937

The 73,295 who turned up to see the Gunners take on Sunderland in
March 1935 were not rewarded with a thrilling performance. A forgettable
match ended 0–0. In contrast, just 39,532 had attended the clash with
Wolverhampton Wanderers three months earlier but they saw a thumping
7–0 victory for Arsenal.

THE 10 HIGHEST HOME ATTENDANCES OVER A SEASON*

	Nos.	Season
1	60,109	2008–09
2	60,062	2007–08
3	60,045	2006–07
4	54,982	1947–48
5	51,478	1948–49
6	51,030	1951–52
7	50,474	1950–51
8	49,191	1952–53
9	49,001	1949–50
10	46,944	1953–54

* Post-war.

	Nos.	Match	Date
1=	100,000	v Liverpool in FA Cup Final	29/4/1950
=	100,000	v Liverpool in FA Cup Final	8/5/1971
3	99,219	v Manchester United in FA Cup Final	12/5/1979
4	96,000	v Liverpool in League Cup Final	5/4/1987
5	93,384	v Sheffield United in FA Cup Final	25/4/1936
6	92,486	v Huddersfield Town in FA Cup Final	26/4/1930
7	92,000	v Liverpool in Charity Shield	11/8/1979
8	91,206	v Cardiff City in FA Cup Final	23/4/1927
9	75,000	v Charlton Athletic in Football League South Cup Final	1/5/1943
10	73,707	v RC Lens in UEFA Champions League group stage	25/11/1998

THE 10 HIGHEST ATTENDANCES FOR THE CHARITY SHIELD

	Nos.	Match	Date
1	92,000	v Liverpool	11/8/1979
2	70,185	V Manchester United	1/8/1999
3	67,342	v Manchester United	9/8/1998
4	67,337	v Liverpool	11/8/2002
5	66,519	v Manchester United	7/8/1993
6	65,483	v Tottenham Hotspur	10/8/1991
7	63,317	v Manchester United	8/8/2004
8	63,149	v Liverpool	12/8/1989
9	59,923	v Manchester United	10/8/2003*
10	58,014	v Chelsea	7/8/2005*

* Community Shield

THE 10 LOWEST HOME
ATTENDANCES (HIGHBURY)

	Nos.	Match	Date
1	4,554	v Leeds United	5/5/1966
2	6,000	v Leicester Fosse	26/12/1914
3=	7,000	v Glossop North End	1/9/1914
=	7,000	v Bristol City	28/11/1914
5	7,233	v Preston North End	26/9/1938
6	8,738	v West Bromwich Albion	5/4/1966
7=	9,000	v Wolverhampton Wanderers	2/1/1915
=	9,000	v Merthyr Town	9/1/1915
9=	10,000	v Fulham	12/9/1914
=	10,000	v Preston North End	12/12/1914
=	10,000	v Nottingham Forest	24/4/1915
=	10,000	v Bolton Wanderers	12/12/1921

PRESENT AND CORRECT

10 OVERSEAS CLUBS WITH ARSENAL-RELATED NAMES

1   Arsenal de Sarandi
Founded in 1957, they compete in the Primera División in Argentina.

2   Arsenal FC Roatan
Founded in 1999, they compete in the Liga de Ascenso de Honduras.

3   Arsenal Klev
Founded in 1934, and renamed in 2001 as Arsenal Kyiv, they compete in the Vyscha Liha in Ukraine.

4   Arsenal Lesotho
They compete in the Lesotho Premier League.

5   Arsenal Wanderers
They compete in the Mauritius Second Division.

6   Berekum Arsenal
Founded in 1978, they compete in the Ghana Telecom Premier League.

7   FC Arsenal Kharkiv
Founded in 1998, they compete in the Druha Liha B in Ukraine.

8   FK Arsenal
Founded in 1919, they compete in the Druga Liga in Montenegro.

9   FK Arsenal Kragujevac
Founded in 1927, they compete in the Serbian league.

10   London City Gunners
Founded in 1996, they compete in Canada's West Region Youth Soccer League.

10 GUNNERS WHO PLAYED IN MAJOR LEAGUE SOCCER IN NORTH AMERICA

	Player	Date played for Arsenal	MLS team and date
1	Alan Ball	1971–76	Vancouver Whitecaps, 1978
2	Geoff Barnett	1969–76	Minnesota Kicks, 1976–80
3	Charlie George	1966–75	Minnesota Kicks, 1978
4	Bill Harper	1925–27, 1930–31	Fall River, 1927–30
5	Joe Haverty	1954–61	Chicago Spurs, 1967
6	Brian Hornsby	1970–76	Edmonton Drillers, 1982
7	Alan Hudson	1976–78	Seattle Sounders, 1978–83
8	Anders Limpar	1990–94	Colorado Rapids, 1999–2000
9	Peter Marinello	1970–73	Phoenix Inferno, 1980–81
10	Peter Simpson	1960–78	New England Teamen 1978–80

TOP 10 AFRICAN
APPEARANCE-MAKERS*

	Player	Country	Games
1	Kolo Toure	Ivory Coast	269
2	Lauren	Cameroon	241
3	Nwankwo Kanu	Nigeria	198
4	Emmanuel Adebayor	Togo	101
5	Emmanuel Eboue	Ivory Coast	100
6	Alexandre Song	Cameroon	25
7	Christopher Wreh	Liberia	46
8	Kaba Diawara	Guinea	12
9	Dan Roux	South Africa	5
10	Carlin Itonga	Congo	1

* Figures correct to the end of January 2009 and do not include substitute
appearances.

TOP 10 SCANDINAVIAN
APPEARANCE-MAKERS*

	Player	Country	Games
1	Freddie Ljungberg	Sweden	328
2	John Jensen	Denmark	129
3	Anders Limpar	Sweden	95
4	Stefan Schwarz	Sweden	49
5	Nicklas Bendtner	Denmark	40
6	Pal Lydersen	Norway	16
7	Sebastian Larsson	Sweden	12
8	Rami Shaaban	Sweden	5
9	Sebastian Svard	Denmark	4
10	Albert Gudmundsson	Iceland	2

* Figures correct to the end of January 2009 and do not include substitute appearances.

TOP 10 FRENCH
APPEARANCE-MAKERS*

	Player	Games
1	Patrick Vieira	406
2	Thierry Henry	370
3	Robert Pires	284
4	Gilles Grimandi	170
5	Sylvain Wiltord	175
6	Mathieu Flamini	153
7	Gael Clichy	119
8	Emmanuel Petit	118
9	Pascal Cygan	98
10	Nicolas Anelka	90

* Figures correct to the end of January 2009. League appearances only.

	Player	Games
1	David O'Leary	722
2	Liam Brady	307
3	Frank Stapleton	300
4	Joe Haverty	122
5	John Devine	111
6	Niall Quinn	94
7	Terry Mancini	62
8	Eddie McGoldrick	57
9	Kevin O'Flanagan	16
10	Paul Gorman	6

Just as the reign of Arsène Wenger has seen a flow of French talent to the Club, so the reign of Terry Neill can be seen as the heyday of Irish and Northern Irish players at Arsenal. Northern Ireland's Sammy Nelson and Pat Rice formed a formidable full-back partnership in front of compatriot Pat Jennings. Other 'green' Gunners during the reign of Ulsterman Neill included Liam Brady, David O'Leary, John Devine and Frank Stapleton.

THE 10 LONGEST-SERVING EMPLOYEES STILL AT THE CLUB

	Name	Job	Started
1=	Ken Friar	Director	1950
=	Pat O'Connor	Ground Staff Stadium Manager	1950
3	Pat Rice	Assistant Manager	1964–80 and 1984
4	Sheila Horne	Manager's Secretary	1970
5	David Miles	Company Secretary	1971
6	Iain Cook	Club Historian	1979
7	Paul Johnson	Equipment Manager	1981
8	Shelley Alger	Secretary to Mr Friar	1983
9=	Vic Akers	First Team Kit Man and Women's Manager	1986
=	Joanne Harney	Publications Office Manager	1986

Note that this is the current job of the employee. Jobs would have changed over the years: for example, Pat Rice started as a 15-year-old apprentice.

10 TALENTED TEENAGERS

1 Tony Adams
The centre back made his debut against Sunderland in November 1983, just four weeks after his 17th birthday.

2 Cliff Bastin
Having signed for Arsenal at 17 in 1929, Bastin was put straight into the first team and won the FA Cup in his first season. He went on to hold the Club's leading-scorer record (178 goals) for over 50 years.

3 Liam Brady
Spotted as a 13-year-old boy by Arsenal scouts, Brady made his first-team debut in 1973 at the age of 17 and quickly became a regular.

4 Cesc Fabregas
The youngest debutant when he played against Rotherham aged 16 years and 177 days, Fabregas became the Club's youngest goalscorer when he netted in the 5–1 victory against Wolverhampton Wanderers on 2 December 2003.

5 Niall Quinn
Quinn was just 19 when he scored on his debut against Liverpool in December 1985.

6 John Radford
Having made his debut when he was 17 years and 28 days, Radford became the Club's youngest ever hat-trick scorer with his three goals against Wolverhampton Wanderers at the age of 17 years and 315 days in 1965.

7 Stewart Robson
In December 1981 Robson made his debut a month after his 17th birthday, becoming a first-team regular before his 18th.

8 Theo Walcott
Walcott was the most expensive 16-year-old in British football history when he signed for the Gunners for a minimum of £5 million. He became the youngest player to appear in European competition for the Club when he appeared at 17 years and 129 days against Dinamo Zagreb in 23 August 2006.

9 Gerry Ward
Ward was the Club's youngest player to appear in a League tie when he faced Huddersfield Town in 1953 at the age of 16 years and 321 days.

10 Jack Wilshere
Ward's record was broken when Wilshere played against Blackburn Rovers at 16 years and 256 days on 13 September 2008.

THE 10 YOUNGEST PREMIER LEAGUE GOALSCORERS

	Player	Age
1	Cesc Fabregas	17 years, 113 days
2	Nicolas Anelka	18 years, 240 days
3	Theo Walcott	18 years, 344 days
4	Jeremie Aliadiere	19 years, 150 days
5	Ray Parlour	19 years, 175 days
6	Ashley Cole	19 years, 264 days
7	John Hartson	19 years, 291 days
8	Abou Diaby	19 years, 325 days
9	Nicklas Bendtner	19 years, 340 days
10	Jermaine Pennant	20 years, 112 days

THE 10 YOUNGEST MEMBERS OF THE 2008–09 SQUAD

	Player	Date of birth
1	Jack Wilshere	1/1/1992
2	Aaron Ramsey	26/12/1990
3	Armand Traore	8/10/1989
4	Theo Walcott	16/3/1989
5	Carlos Vela	1/3/1989
6	Vito Mannone	2/3/1988
7	Denilson	16/2/1988
8	Nicklas Bendtner	16/1/1988
9	Alex Song	9/9/1987
10	Cesc Fabregas	4/5/1987

FIRST 10 HONOURS
WON BY ARSENAL LADIES

	Trophy	Year
1	FA Women's Premier League Cup	1992
2	FA Women's Premier League Cup	1993
3	FA Women's Cup	1993
4	FA Women's Premier League	1993
5	FA Women's Premier League Cup	1994
6	FA Women's Premier League	1995
7	FA Women's Cup	1995
8	FA Women's Premier League	1997
9	FA Women's Premier League Cup	1998
10	FA Women's Cup	1998

THE 10 MOST-CAPPED
ARSENAL LADIES

	Player	Caps
1	Rachel Yankey	85
2	Kelly Smith	76
3	Ciara Grant (Republic of Ireland)	65
4	Faye White	63
5	Katie Chapman	62
6	Emma Byrne (Republic of Ireland)	60
7	Jayne Ludlow (Wales)	42
8	Karen Carney	41
9	Alex Scott	40
10	Laura Bassett	9

10 AWARDS WON
BY ARSENAL LADIES

	Player	Award	Year
1	Faye White	Women's Premier League Player of the Year	1998
2	Kelly Smith	Women's International Player of the Year	2005
3	Rachel Yankey	Nationwide International Player of the Year	2005
4	Rachel Yankey	MBE	2005
5	Ciara Grant	Women's International Player of the Year	2006
6	Kelly Smith	Nationwide Players' Player of the Year	2006
7	Arsenal Ladies	The Committee Award in the Sports Journalists' Awards	2007
8	Karen Carney	FA National Young Player of the Year	2007
9	Faye White	MBE	2007
10	Kelly Smith	MBE	2008

THE FAIRER SEX

TOP 10 MANAGERIAL-REIGN GOAL TALLIES DURING HIGHBURY ERA*

	Manager	Goals
1	Herbert Chapman	460
2	Tom Whittaker	458
3	Arsène Wenger	420
4	Bertie Mee	324
5	George Graham	307
6	George Allison	290
7	Terry Neill	249
8	Leslie Knighton	186
9	Billy Wright	178
10	George Swindin	175

* League matches only.

	Average	Season
1	2.29	2001–02
2	2.28	2004–05
3	2.23	2002–03
4	1.94	2007–08
5=	1.92	1999–2000
=	1.92	2003–04
7	1.79	2005–06
8	1.78	1997–98
9	1.66	2006–07
10	1.55	1998–99

THE 10 HIGHEST GOAL AVERAGES AGAINST TOP-HALF PREMIERSHIP TEAMS

	Average	Season
1	2.27	2004–05
2	1.88	2006–07
3	1.83	2002–03
4	1.77	2001–02
5	1.70	1999–2000
6	1.66	1998–99
7	1.56	2003–04
8	1.55	2007–08
9	1.50	1997–98
10	1.22	2000–01

Season 2004–05 tops this list thanks, in the main, to two high-scoring games against Middlesbrough and Tottenham Hotspur. The Gunners beat Middlesbrough – who eventually finished seventh – 5–3 on 22/8/2004, and overcame Tottenham – who finished ninth – 5–4 on 13/11/2004.

THE 10 HIGHEST-SCORING
GUNNERS AT
INTERNATIONAL LEVEL*

	Player	Country	Goals
1	Thierry Henry	France	48
2	Davor Suker	Croatia	45
3	Dennis Bergkamp	Netherlands	37
4	Emmanuel Adebayor	Togo	34
5	David Platt	England	27
6	Sylvain Wiltord	France	26
7	Frank Stapleton	Republic of Ireland	20
8	Marc Overmars	Netherlands	17
9	Tony Woodcock	England	16
10=	John Hartson	Wales	14
=	Freddie Ljungberg	Sweden	14
=	Robert Pires	France	14

* Figures correct to the end of January 2009.

THE 10 HIGHEST GOALKEEPERS' CLEAN-SHEET RATIOS*

	Goalkeeper	Appearance	Clean sheets	%
1	David Seaman	564	237	42
2=	Manuel Almunia	129	53	41
=	Bob Wilson	308	125	41
4	Jens Lehmann	199	79	40
5	John Lukic	298	114	38
6=	Jock Robson	101	37	37
=	George Wood	70	26	37
8	James Ashcroft	303	108	36
9	Joe Lievesley	75	26	35
10=	Alex Manninger	64	22	34
=	Frank Moss	161	55	34

* This list is drawn from goalkeepers with over 50 appearances.

10 GOALSCORERS
WHO HAVE SCORED FOR AND AGAINST THE CLUB

	Player	Match and score	Date
1	Nicolas Anelka	Arsenal 2–1 Bolton Wanderers	14/4/2001
2	Kevin Campbell	Arsenal 1–1 Nottingham Forest	28/8/1995
3	Lee Chapman	Leeds United 3–0 Arsenal	21/11/1992
4	Eduardo	Arsenal 2–1 Dinamo Zagreb	23/8/2006
5	Nwankwo Kanu	Arsenal 3–1 Portsmouth	2/9/2007
6	Paul Merson	Arsenal 3–2 Aston Villa	9/12/2001
7	Charlie Nicholas	Arsenal 2–2 Celtic	30/7/1991
8	Emmanuel Petit	Arsenal 3–2 Chelsea	1/1/2003
9	Niall Quinn	Sunderland 1–0 Arsenal	19/8/2000
10	Tomas Rosicky	Arsenal 4–2 Sparta Prague	25/1/2000

FIRST 10 TEAMS
THIERRY HENRY
SCORED AGAINST

	Match	Date	Goals
1	Southampton (a)	19/9/1999	1
2	AIK Solna (Wembley)	22/9/1999	1
3	Derby County (h)	28/11/1999	2
4	Middlesbrough (a)	30/11/1999	1
5	Nantes (a)	9/12/1999	1
6	Wimbledon (h)	18/12/1999	1
7	Leeds United (h)	28/12/1999	1
8	Sunderland (h)	15/1/2000	2
9	Bradford City (a)	5/2/2000	1
10	Deportivo (h)	2/3/2000	1

10 THIERRY HENRY
SCORING FACTS*

1   **110** were scored in a Premiership match with his right foot.

2   **101** were scored inside the penalty box from open play in Premiership ties.

3   **99** were scored at home in a Premiership tie.

4   **43** were scored away from home in the Premiership.

5   **37** were scored between the 76th and 90th minute of Premiership ties.

6   **26** were scored with his left foot in the UEFA Champions League.

7   **21** were scored inside the penalty box from open play in the UEFA Champions League.

8   **19** were scored between the 61st and 75th minute in Premiership ties.

9   **17** were scored at home in the UEFA Champions League.

10   **14** were scored outside the area in open play in Premiership ties.

* These statistics cover his first 186 goals for the Club – the goals that secured his place as top goalscorer.

TOP 10 ASSIST-MAKERS
IN THE 2007-08 SEASON

	Player	Assists
1	Cesc Fabregas	?3
2	Alexander Hleb	14
3	Eduardo	10
4=	Gael Clichy	7
=	Theo Walcott	7
6=	Nicklas Bendtner	6
=	Bacary Sagna	6
8=	Emmanuel Adebayor	5
=	Robin van Persie	5
10	Kolo Toure	4

10 MEMORABLE PENALTIES

1   **Juan Roman Riquelme, Villarreal v Arsenal, 25 April 2006**
    The Gunners were seconds from their first UEFA Champions League
    final when the Spaniards were awarded a spot-kick that threatened
    to deny them. Jens Lehmann was the hero of the hour with his save.

2   **Attilio Lombardo, Sampdoria v Arsenal, 20 April 1995**
    The climax of a spectacular evening in Genoa saw David Seaman
    dive to his left and save the bald winger's shot and send Arsenal to
    their second successive European Cup Winners' Cup Final.

3   **Lauren, Arsenal v Tottenham Hotspur, 6 April 2002**
    Teddy Sheringham's spot-kick seven minutes from time had
    cancelled Ljungberg's opener, threatening to derail the Gunners'
    title charge. With regular penalty-taker Henry being treated off the
    pitch, the defender stood up and sealed a crucial victory.

4   **Sylvain Wiltord, Arsenal v Rotherham United,
    28 October 2003**
    The Frenchman missed the first spot-kick of this epic tie but made
    no mistake ten penalties later, with the conclusive penalty of the
    shoot-out that Arsenal won 9–8.

5   **David Seaman, Arsenal v Manchester United, 7 August 1993**
    A case of 'gamekeeper turned poacher' here as the Yorkshireman
    stepped up to take a penalty against Peter Schmeichel in the
    Charity Shield shoot-out. Sadly he missed and the Shield went to
    Old Trafford.

6 Peter Storey, Arsenal v Stoke City, 27 March 1971

Here too the Club's dream of the double was kept alive by a penalty. Having trailed 2–0 to Stoke, they finished the game at 2–2 thanks to two Storey goals, the latter from the penalty spot.

7 Thierry Henry, Arsenal v Wigan Athletic, 7 May 2006

Thierry Henry completed a hat-trick, confirmed the Club's UEFA Champions League qualification and scored the final goal at Highbury all with one stroke of his boot.

8 Thierry Henry and Robert Pires, Arsenal v Manchester City, 22 October 2005

From a penalty we never want to forget to one we wish we could. Trying to pull off a clever trick, Pires fluffed his attempted pass to Henry, who watched confused. But not half as confused as the spectators.

9 Dennis Bergkamp, Arsenal v Manchester United, 14 April 1999

In the final minute of this FA Cup semi-final replay, the Dutchman's effort was saved by Peter Schmeichel. United went on to win the tie and, indeed, the Treble.

10 Ruud van Nistlerooy, Manchester United v Arsenal, 21 September 2003

At the end of a highly charged tie, the Dutchman smacked his effort against the crossbar, prompting memorable scenes.

THE 10 HIGHEST-SCORING
CHAMPIONSHIP SEASONS*

	Season	Goals
1	1930–31	127
2	1932–33	118
3	1934–35	115
4	1952–53	97
5	1947–48	81
6	2001–02	79
7	1937–38	77
8	1933–34	75
9	1990–91	74
10=	1988–89	73
=	2003–04	73

* League goals only.

SCORING, SCORING ARSENAL

THE 10 FASTEST PLAYERS
TO SCORE 100 GOALS

	Player	Games
1	Ted Drake	108
2	Ian Wright	143
3	Jimmy Brain	144
4	Jack Lambert	149
5=	Reg Lewis	152
=	Joe Baker	152
7	David Jack	156
8	Doug Lishman	163
9	David Herd	165
10	Cliff Bastin	174

10 GREAT GOAL
CELEBRATIONS

1 Charlie George v Liverpool, May 1971
This iconic celebration saw George fall to the ground and lie on his back with a combination of exhaustion and relief after scoring the winner in the FA Cup Final at a blazing Wembley.

2 Brian Kidd v Manchester City, August 1974
In front of the adoring North Bank, Kidd celebrated his goal by taking the helmet from a policeman and putting it on his own head.

3 Sammy Nelson v Coventry City, April 1979
Having put the visitors ahead with an own goal, Nelson was mightily relieved to equalize in front of the North Bank. So much so, he dropped his shorts and bared his backside.

4 Dennis Bergkamp v Tottenham Hotspur, November 1996
The Gunners sealed a 3–1 victory in the final minutes of this tie thanks to goals from Tony Adams and Bergkamp. The Dutchman celebrated his goal by sliding on his knees and roaring in front of the ecstatic North Bank.

5 Dennis Bergkamp (and team-mates) v Sunderland, January 1997
After scoring a magnificent goal involving a double-dragback and a fine lob, the Dutchman clasped his hand to his mouth and giggled. His team-mates soon matched this.

6   Ian Wright v Bolton Wanderers, September 1997
When he scored his 178th goal for Arsenal, to equal Cliff Bastin's record. Wright removed his shirt to reveal a T-shirt with the slogan '179 – just done it'. Unfortunately he was still one goal away from that target, but happily he scored twice more in the same game.

7   Tony Adams v Everton, May 1998
The centre back lashed home a fine left-footed volley to seal this title-winning victory. His arms-outstretched response was both understated and iconic.

8   Nwankwo Kanu v Middlesbrough, April 1999
The Nigerian responded like a true Gunner to his wonder strike by forming an imaginary gun with his hand and coolly blowing the smoke from its barrel.

9   Thierry Henry v Tottenham Hotspur, November 2002
Having run for 65 metres (70 yards) and then netted in front of the North Bank, the Frenchman decided to run the entire length of the pitch again and slid on to his knees in front of the crestfallen visiting supporters.

10   Theo Walcott v Slavia Prague, October 2007
In a touching celebration, Walcott point to the sky, later explaining that this was in tribute to his brother-in-law's brother, who had recently passed away.

TOP 10 GOALSCORERS

Player		Goals
1	Thierry Henry	226
2	Ian Wright	185
3	Cliff Bastin	178
4	John Radford	149
5=	Jimmy Brain	139
=	Ted Drake	139
7	Doug Lishman	137
8	Joe Hulme	125
9	David Jack	124
10	Reg Lewis	116

SCORING, SCORING ARSENAL

TOP 10 GOALSCORERS
IN A SEASON

	Player	Goals	Season
1	Ted Drake	43	1934–35
2=	Jack Lambert	39	1930–31
=	Thierry Henry	39	2003 04
4	Jimmy Brain	37	1925–26
5	Ian Wright	35	1993–94
6	Jimmy Brain	34	1926–27
7=	Ronnie Rooke	33	1947–48
=	Cliff Bastin	33	1932–33
=	Thierry Henry	33	2005–06
10=	Thierry Henry	32	2001–02
=	Thierry Henry	32	2002–03

10 ONE-GOAL WONDERS

	Player	Appearances	Season
1	Jeff Blockley	62	1972–73, 1974–75
2	Bill Dodgin	207	1952–53, 1959–61
3	Don Howe	74	1964–65, 1966–67
4	John Jensen	137	1992–96
5	Archie Macaulay	107	1947–50
6	Eddie McGoldrick	56	1993–96
7	Terry Mancini	62	1974–76
8	Frank Moss	159	1931–37
9	Colin Pates	27	1989–90, 1992–93
10	Nelson Vivas	69	1998–99, 2000–01

SCORING, SCORING ARSENAL

THE 10 HIGHEST GOAL-DIFFERENCE CAMPAIGNS

	Season	Goal difference
1=	1903–04	69
=	1934–35	69
3	1930–31	68
4	1932–33	57
5	1990–91	56
6	1947–48	49
7	2003–04	47
8=	2001–02	43
=	2002–03	43
10	1970–71	42

10 HIGH-SCORING
CHRISTMAS DAY MATCHES

	Match and score	Year
1	Woolwich Arsenal 5–0 Preston Hornets	1889
2	Sheffield United 3–3 Arsenal	1891
3	Arsenal 4–1 Burslem PV	1893
4	Woolwich Arsenal 7–0 Burslem PV	1894
5	Woolwich Arsenal 6–2 Lincoln City	1896
6	Lincoln City 5–0 Arsenal	1899
7	Woolwich Arsenal 4–3 Newcastle United	1902
8	Everton 4–2 Arsenal	1920
9	Arsenal 5–3 Preston North End	1934
10	Bolton Wanderers 4–6 Arsenal	1952

SCORING, SCORING ARSENAL

10 HAT-TRICK SCORERS

	Player	Hat-tricks
1	Jack Lambert	12
2	Jimmy Brain	11
3	Ian Wright	11
4	Ted Drake	9
5	Doug Lishman	9
6	Thierry Henry	8
7	David Herd	7
8	David Jack	7
9	John Radford	6
10	Joe Baker	5

TOP 10 LEAGUE GOALSCORERS
AT HIGHBURY

	Player	Goals
1	Thierry Henry	114
2=	Cliff Bastin	88
=	Doug Lishman	88
4	Jimmy Brain	80
5	Ted Drake	74
6	Ian Wright	71
7	Joe Hulme	66
8	John Radford	65
9	David Herd	63
10	Reg Lewis	61

Henry not only holds the honour of being the top goalscorer at Highbury, he also has the distinction of scoring the final goal and the final hat-trick at the stadium. Both came against Wigan Athletic on 7/5/2006. He completed his hat-trick from the penalty spot and kissed the turf to celebrate.

10 HAT-TRICK SCORERS
AT HIGHBURY*

	Player	Hat-tricks
1	Jimmy Brain	11
2	Thierry Henry	7
3	Jack Lambert	7
4	Doug Lishman	7
5	Ted Drake	6
6	Ian Wright	6
7	David Herd	5
8	David Jack	5
9	Ronnie Rooke	5
10	John Radford	4

* Refers to total number of hat-tricks scored by the players at Highbury only.

10 EMIRATES STADIUM STATS

1   **12,000** light fittings
2   **4,500** IT/data points
3   **4,500** metal handrails
4   **900** toilets
5   **439** high-definition screens
6   **130** CCTV cameras
7   **56** roof speakers
8   **41** TV camera positions
9   **2** sprinkler tanks
10 **2** cannons

THE 10 TALLEST
GUNNERS

	Player	Height
1=	Niall Quinn	1.95m (6ft 5in)
=	Stuart Taylor	1.95m (6ft 5in)
3	Mart Poom	1.94m (6ft 4½in)
4=	Steve Bould	1.93m (6ft 4in)
=	Pascal Cygan	1.93m (6ft 4in)
=	Jim Fotheringham	1.93m (6ft 4in)
=	John Lukic	1.93m (6ft 4in)
=	Rami Shaaban	1.93m (6ft 4in)
=	Igor Stepanovs	1.93m (6ft 4in)
=	Patrick Vieira	1.93m (6ft 4in)

THE 10 HEAVIEST
IN THE 2008–09 SQUAD

	Player	Weight
1	Johan Djourou	88.9kg (14st)
2=	Manuel Almunia	85.7kg (13st 7lb)
=	Mikael Silvestre	85.7kg (13st 7lb)
4=	Nicklas Bendtner	82.5kg (13st)
=	Lucas Fabianski	82.5kg (13st)
6	Mark Randall	81.6kg (12st 12lb)
7=	Vito Mannone	76.2kg (12st)
=	Kolo Toure	76.2kg (12st)
9=	Abou Diaby	74.8kg (11st 11lb)
=	Samir Nasri	74.8kg (11st 11lb)

WEIGHTS AND MEASURES

10 GUNNERS TO CAPTAIN
THEIR COUNTRY

	Player	**Country**
1	Tony Adams	England
2	Alan Ball	England
3	Eddie Hapgood	England
4	Thierry Henry	France
5	David Jack	England
6	Nwankwo Kanu	Nigeria
7	George Male	England
8	David Platt	England
9	David Seaman	England
10	Patrick Vieira	France

10 GREAT INTERNATIONAL CONTRIBUTIONS

1 **Patrick Vieira and Emmanuel Petit at the 1998 World Cup**
On home soil, the Gunners midfielders were key to their nation's winning campaign, even combining to score the crowning goal of the Final.

2 **David Seaman at the 1996 European Championship**
The goalkeeper saved a penalty at a pivotal moment in the clash with Scotland and was a national hero when his penalty save in the shoot-out against Spain sent England to the semi-finals.

3 **The 'Arsenal Seven' for England v Italy in 1934**
The Club provided seven of the starting 11 for this bruising clash with the then world champions.

4 **Thierry Henry, Patrick Vieira, Sylvain Wiltord, Robert Pires and Emmanuel Petit at the 2000 European Championship**
The Gunners contingent formed a key part of the team that followed up on its World Cup triumph by winning the Euros. Henry was top scorer of the tournament.

5 **Lauren at the 2000 Olympic Games**
The defender had been present when Cameroon won the Africa Cup of Nations earlier in 2000. The Final of the Olympics went to penalties and he duly scored the fourth as his nation won the shoot-out 5–3.

6 **Dave Bowen at the 1958 World Cup**
Skippered his Welsh side to the quarter-finals in their only World Cup campaign to date. There they faced Brazil and the defender was inspirational as he faced a 17-year-old called Pelé.

7 **David O'Leary at the 1990 World Cup**
The Irishman was not known for his goalscoring from the penalty spot or anywhere else. However, he expertly stroked the crucial spot-kick that sent Jack Charlton's team to the quarter-finals.

8 **Theo Walcott v Croatia in 2008**
The Arsenal youngster made the world sit up and take notice with his hat-trick in this World Cup qualifier.

9 **Cesc Fabregas at the 2008 European Championship**
The young Spaniard scored twice and set up two goals as Spain marched to the Final, where he was again a key figure in his nation's victory.

10 **Gilberto at the 2007 Copa America**
The midfielder had won the World Cup with Brazil the summer before he became a Gunner. At the Copa America he was captain of the winning nation and even scored from the spot in the semi-final shoot-out against Uruguay.

THE 10 MOST-CAPPED
ENGLAND PLAYERS*

	Player	Caps
1	Kenny Sansom	77
2	Sol Campbell	73
3=	Alan Ball	72
=	David Seaman	72
5	Tony Adams	66
6	David Platt	62
7	Ashley Cole	51
8	Martin Keown	43
9	Ian Wright	33
10	Viv Anderson	30

* For some players not all their cups were won as an Arsenal player. Figures correct to the end of January 2009.

THE 10 MOST-CAPPED
PLAYERS*

	Player	Country	Caps
1	Thierry Henry	France	80
2=	Dennis Bergkamp	Holland	79
=	Patrick Vieira	France	79
4	Kenny Sansom	England	77
5	Sol Campbell	England	73
6	David Seaman	England	72
=	Alan Ball	England	72
8	David O'Leary	Republic of Ireland	68
9	Tony Adams	England	66
10	Freddie Ljungberg	Sweden	60

* Figures correct to the end of January 2009.

10 INTERNATIONAL MEDAL-WINNING GUNNERS

	Player	**Medals**
1	Thierry Henry	World Cup, 1998; European Championship, 2000
2	Emmanuel Petit	World Cup, 1998; European Championship, 2000
3	Robert Pires	World Cup, 1998; European Championship, 2000
4	Patrick Vieira	World Cup, 1998; European Championship, 2000
5	Sylvain Wiltord	World Cup, 1998; European Championship, 2000
6	Lauren	Africa Cup of Nations, 2000; Olympic Games, 2000
7	Gilberto	World Cup 2002; Copa America, 2004
8	Alan Ball	World Cup, 1966
9	Julio Baptista	Copa America, 2004
10	Cesc Fabregas	European Championship, 2008

IF THE CAP FITS

10 HOME NATIONS
ONE-CAP WONDERS

	Player	Match	Date
1	John Coleman	England v Northern Ireland	1907
2	Alex Graham	Scotland v Northern Ireland	1921
3	John Butler	England v Belgium	1924
4	Alf Baker	England v Wales	1927
5	Herdie Roberts	England v Scotland	1931
6	Bernard Joy	England v Belgium	1936
7	Arthur Milton	England v Austria	1951
8	Jimmy Logie	Scotland v Northern Ireland	1952
9	Danny Clapton	England v Wales	1958
10	Jeff Blockley	England v Yugoslavia	1972

THE 10 MOST-CAPPED ENGLAND PLAYERS UNDER GEORGE GRAHAM

	Player	Caps
1	Tony Adams	31
2	Lee Dixon	21
3	Kenny Sansom	15
4=	Paul Merson	14
=	David Rocastle	14
=	Ian Wright	14
7	Alan Smith	13
8	David Seaman	11
9	Viv Anderson	6
10=	Steve Bould	2
=	Martin Keown	2
=	Michael Thomas	2
=	Nigel Winterburn	2

TOP 10 LEAGUE TEAMS
OF THE 20TH CENTURY*

	Club	Position
1	Arsenal	8.5
2	Liverpool	0.7
3	Everton	10.6
4	Manchester United	10.9
5	Aston Villa	12.5
6	Tottenham Hotspur	13.2
7	Newcastle United	14.4
8	Manchester City	14.5
9	Chelsea	15.4
10	Sunderland	16.6

* Figures based on the average League finishes of clubs between 1900 and 1999.

10 GUNNERS TO RECEIVE CIVILIAN HONOURS

	Player	Honour	Year
1	Denis Compton	CBE	1958
2	Billy Wright	CBE	1972
3	Bertie Mee	OBE	1972
4	Frank McLintock	MBE	1972
5	George Eastham	OBE	1973
6	Joe Mercer	OBE	1976
7	Pat Jennings	MBE; OBE	1976; 1987
8	Arfon Griffiths	MBE	1977
9	John Hollins	MBE	1982
10	David Seaman	MBE	1997

TOP 10 GUNNERS
AS VOTED BY
ARSENAL PLAYERS*

	Player	Votes
1	Patrick Vieira	45
2	Tony Adams	43
3=	Liam Brady	42
=	Thierry Henry	42
5=	George Armstrong	29
=	Kenny Sansom	29
7	Pat Jennings	28
8	Frank McLintock	25
9	Robert Pires	24
10	Ian Wright	22

* 52 prominent Arsenal players were asked to vote for their ultimate Arsenal team.
The players above received the highest number of votes.

TOP 10 FOOTBALL LEAGUE LEGENDS*

	Player	Appearances
1	Eddie Hapgood	440
2	Frank McLintock	403
3	Cliff Bastin	392
4	Dennis Bergkamp	346
5	Pat Jennings	326
6	Liam Brady	306
7	Joe Mercer	273
8	Alex James	259
9	David Jack	208
10	Ted Drake	184

* As part of the Football League centenary celebrations, 100 Football League Legends were named in August 1998. Any player, of any nationality, who had played in the Football League or the FA Premier League was eligible for inclusion.

FIRST 10 PLAYERS TO APPEAR IN THE PFA'S TEAM OF THE YEAR*

	Player	Year
1	Tony Adams	1996
2=	David Seaman	1997
=	Ian Wright	1997
4	Dennis Bergkamp	1998
5=	Emmanuel Petit	1999
=	Patrick Vieira	1999, 2000, 2002, 2003
=	Nicolas Anelka	1999
8=	Silvinho	2001
=	Thierry Henry	2001, 2002
10	Robert Pires	2002, 2003

* Every year, members of the Professional Footballers' Association vote for their Team of the Year.

FIRST 10 WINNERS OF THE OFFICIAL SUPPORTERS CLUB PLAYER OF THE YEAR

	Player	Year
1	Frank McLintock	1967
2	John Radford	1968
3	Peter Simpson	1969
4	George Armstrong	1970
5	Bob Wilson	1971
6	Pat Rice	1972
7	John Radford	1973
8	Alan Ball	1974
9	Jimmy Rimmer	1975
10	Liam Brady	1976

AWARDS AND HONOURS

10 PLAYER AWARDS
WON BY THIERRY HENRY

Award	Year
1	French Player of the Year	2000, 2003, 2004, 2005, 2006
2	Premier League Golden Boot	2002, 2004, 2005, 2006
3	Named in Premier League Overseas Team of the Decade	2003
4	PFA Players' Player of the Year	2003, 2004
5	Football Writers' Player of the Year	2003, 2004, 2006
6	Named as one of the Association of Football Statisticians Greatest Ever Footballers	2004
7	Named as one of Pelé's 125 Greatest Living Footballers	2004
8	European Golden Boot	2004, 2005
9	Named as favourite Premier League Player of All Time in Barclays survey	2008
10	Named as Greatest Ever Arsenal Player of All Time by Arsenal.com users	2008

	Player	Year
1	Liam Brady	1979
2	Tony Adams	1987
3	Paul Merson	1989
4	Dennis Bergkamp	1998
5	Nicolas Anelka	1999
6	Niall Quinn	2002
7	Thierry Henry	2003
8	Thierry Henry	2003
9	Thierry Henry	2004
10	Thierry Henry	2004

* Every year, members of the Professional Footballers' Association vote for their Player of the Year and Young Player of the Year. Adams, Merson, Anelka and Fabregas were voted Young Player of the Year, the others Player of the Year. Niall Quinn won PFA's Special Merit Award and, in addition to Player of the Year, Henry won PFA Fans' Player of the Year in 2003 and 2004.

THE 10 MOST COMMON
PLAYERS' FIRST NAMES*

1   **John (and Johnny, Jon)** 17 Barnwell, Devine, Dick, Halls, Hartson, Hawley, Jensen, Kosmina, Lukic, Matthews, Petts, Radford, Roberts, Sammels, Snedden, Spicer, Woodward

2   **David** 14 Bentley, Cork, Court, Grondin, Herd, Hillier, Jack, Jenkins, Madden, O'Leary, Platt, Price, Rocastle, Seaman

3   **Jimmy (and James, Jim)** 13 Ashcroft, Bloomfield, Brain, Carter, Fotheringham, Furnell, Harvey, Logie, McGill, Magill, Rimmer, Robertson, Standen

4   **George** 10 Armstrong, Eastham, Ford, Graham, Grant, Johnston, Male, Morrell, Swindin, Wood

5= **Frank (and Francesc, Francis, Frankie)** 9 Bradshaw, Cownley, Fabregas, Jeffers, McLintock, Moss, O'Neill, Simek, Stapleton

=   **Paul** 9 Barron, Davies, Davis, Dickov, Gorman, Mariner, Merson, Shaw, Vaessen

=   **Tom (and Tomas, Tommy)** 9 Black, Caton, Coakley, Danilevicius, Docherty, Lawton, Parker, Rosicky, Walley

8   **Alan** 8 Ball, Hudson, Miller, Skirton, Smith, Sunderland, Tyrer, Young

9= **Jack** 6 Butler, Crayston, Flanagan, Lambert, McClelland, Wilshere

=   **Joe** 6 Haverty, Hulme, Lievesley, North, Shaw, Toner

=   **Steve** 6 Bould, Brignall, Dunn, Gatting, Hughes, Morrow

* Covering players who have appeared in at least one Arsenal match since World War II.

10 'ONE-OFF' FIRST NAMES

1 **Abou** Diaby
2 **Fabian** Caballero
3 **Gilles** Grimandi
4 **Jens** Lehmann
5 **Junichi** Inamoto
6 **Mel** Charles
7 **Nwankwo** Kanu
8 **Pascal** Cygan
9 **Quincy** Owusu-Abeyie
10 **Rami** Shaaban

WHAT'S IN A NAME?

10 LONG-NAMED ARSENAL PLAYERS*

1 Giovanni van Bronckhorst
2 Quincy Owusu-Abeyie
3 Michal Papadopulos
4 Emmanuel Adebayor
5 Jose Antonio Reyes
6 Philippe Senderos
7 Lukasz Fabianski
8 Jim Fotheringham
9 Mikael Silvestre
10 Robin van Persie

* Covers Arsenal players from the 1950–51 season onwards.

When Giovanni van Bronckhorst – whose full name is Giovanni Christiaan van Bronckhorst – signed in 2001, vice-chairman David Dein joked, "We nearly didn't sign him because the letters didn't fit on the back of his shirt."

10 MEMORABLE
MIDDLE NAMES

1. Caesar **Augustus Llewelyn** Jenkins
2. David **Carlyle** Rocastle
3. Gus **Cassius** Caesar
4. Charlie **James Fane** Preedy
5. Sol **Jeremiah** Campbell
6. Michael **Lauriston** Thomas
7. Bob **Primrose** Wilson
8. David **Reno** Bacuzzi
9. Archibald **Renwick** Macaulay
10. Alex **Rooney** Forbes

10 ALLITERATIVELY NAMED PLAYERS*

1   Brendon Batson

2   Billy Blyth

3   Francesc Fàbregas

4   George Grant

5   George Graham

6   Gilles Grimandi

7   John Jensen

8   Malcolm Macdonald

9   Stefan Schwarz

10 Sebastian Svard

* Covers Arsenal players from the 1950–51 season onwards.

10 PLAYERS' NICKNAMES

	Player	Nickname
1	Viv Anderson	Spider*
2	Liam Brady	Chippy
3	Eddie Clamp	Chopper
4	Malcolm Macdonald	Supermac
5	Marc Ovemars	Roadrunner
6	Ray Parlour	Romford Pelé
7	David Rocastle	Rocky
8	David Seaman	Safe Hands
9	Alan Skirton	Highbury Express
10	Bob Wilson	Willow

* As well as Anderson, David O'Leary and Charlie Preedy were known by this nickname in the dressing room.

THE 10 MOST COMMON INITIALS FOR PLAYERS' SURNAMES*

	Initial	Number of surnames
1	S	33
2	M	28
3	B	27
4	H	25
=	C	25
6	G	21
7	W	19
8	R	18
9	D	16
10=	A	11
=	P	11

* Covers Arsenal players from the 1950–51 season onwards.

10 ARSENAL-SUPPORTING MEMBERS OF TEAM GB AT THE 2008 OLYMPIC GAMES

	Competitor	Sport
1	Blake Aldridge	Diving
2	Tyrone Edgar	Athletics: 100 metres
3	Mo Farah	Athletics: 5,000 metres
4	Joe Glanfield	Sailing (silver medal)
5	Richard Kruse	Fencing
6	Germaine Mason	Athletics: high jump (silver medal)
7	Dean Milwain	Swimming
8	Alex O'Connell	Fencing
9	Victoria Pendleton	Cycling (gold medal)
10	Kelly Sotherton	Heptathlon

10 REQUIREMENTS TO QUALIFY AS AN OFFICIAL SUPPORTERS CLUB

1   The aim must be to bring together like-minded Arsenal supporters in the region.

2   The supporters club must consist of at least 50 members.

3   A chairperson, secretary and treasurer must be appointed.

4   Two personal character references must be submitted for each of these three.

5   There must be no other Arsenal supporters club within a 80-kilometre (50-mile) radius.

6   The supporters club must hold at least three committee meetings per season.

7   The supporters club must hold an annual general meeting.

8   All members must be invited to the annual general meeting.

9   Annual accounts for the supporters club must be produced at the annual general meeting.

10 The supporters club must have access to a minimum of one computer with Internet and email facilities.

10 KEY JUNIOR GUNNERS
MOMENTS

	Event	Date
1	Future Junior Gunners member (and Arsenal first-team star) **Ashley Cole** born	December 1980
2	**Junior Gunners** launched in match-day programme for Arsenal v Luton Town	August 1983
3	**Daniel Quy** becomes first Junior Gunners mascot	August 1983
4	**Mascot Gunnersaurus** 'born' in the North Bank	August 1993
5	**Daniel Quy** appointed Assistant Manager of the Junior Gunners	May 1994
6	**Arsenal Soccer Schools** launched in Thailand	September 2002
7	Junior Gunner **Luke Patel** presents Arsène Wenger with a set of glasses to celebrate his birthday	October 2005
8	**First Junior Gunners Forum,** with members quizzing Cesc Fabregas and Johan Djourou about a range of topics	February 2006
9	**First Junior Gunners Christmas party,** when fans got to watch the players train, held at Emirates Stadium	December 2006
10	**Ken Banham Tournament,** with young football teams each including at least one Junior Gunner	April 2007

10 UK REGIONS
WITH LARGEST NUMBER
OF ARSENAL FANS*

	Region	Supporters
1	London	158,484
2	South East	134,028
3	East of England	124,064
4	South West	33,869
5	East Midlands	20,387
6	West Midlands	15,790
7	Yorkshire and the Humber	12,188
8	North West	11,601
9	Wales	9,810
10	Northern Ireland	9,188

* Covers official members, tour purchasers and people who have purchased merchandise up to January 2009.

10 ARSENAL-SUPPORTING
TELEVISION PERSONALITIES

	Personality	TV programme/character
1	Melvyn Bragg	*South Bank Show*
2	Kathy Burke	*Harry Enfield Show*
3	Alan Davis	*QI*
4	Paul Kaye*	*Dennis Pennis*
5	Matt Lucas	*Little Britain*
6	Davina McCall	*Big Brother*
7	Rory McGrath	*They Think It's All Over*
8	Dermot O'Leary	*X Factor, Big Brother*
9	Linda Robson	*Birds of a Feather*
10	Bradley Walsh	*Wheel of Fortune, National Lottery*

* See page 202 for Paul Kaye's list of 10 Moments Guaranteed to Make you Smile.

10 ARSENAL-SUPPORTING MUSICAL FOLK

Musician

1   **Marc Almond** (Soft Cell)

2   **Roger Daltrey** (The Who)

3   **Ray Davies** (The Kinks)

4   **Dido**

5   **Tony Hadley** (Spandau Ballet)

6   **Chris Lowe** (Pet Shop Boys)

7   **John Lydon** (Sex Pistols, PiL)

8   **Sharleen Spiteri** (Texas)

9   **Rachel Stevens** (S Club 7)

10 **Pete Tong**

	Sportsperson	Sport
1	James Anderson	Cricket
2	Stuart Barnes	Rugby
3	Martin Brundle	Formula One
4	Thomas Castaignede	Rugby Union
5	Frankie Dettori	Horseracing
6	Ronnie O'Sullivan	Snooker
7	Ian Poulter	Golf
8	Ferenc Puskas	Football
9	Daley Thompson	Athletics
10	Phil Tufnell	Cricket

Ferenc Puskas read about Herbert Chapman's Arsenal in Hungarian newspapers. He said, "There was only one side for me – Arsenal." Puskas was photographed in an Arsenal shirt, playing keepy-uppy alongside England goalkeeper Gordon Banks.

10 ARSENAL-SUPPORTING
EASTENDERS STARS

	Actor	Character
1	James Alexandrou	Martin Fowler
2	Gary Beadle	Paul Trueman
3	Leonard Fenton	Dr Legg
4	Michelle Gayle	Hattie Tavernier
5	Mark Homer	Tony Hills
6	Patsy Palmer	Bianca Butcher
7	Gillian Taylforth	Kathy Beale
8	Jessie Wallace	Kat Moon
9	Tom Watt	Lofty Holloway
10	Barbara Windsor	Peggy Mitchell

10 ARSENAL-SUPPORTING BOXERS

	Boxer	Title
1	Nicky Cook	European Featherweight Champion
2	Sir Henry Cooper	former British and Empire Heavyweight Champion
3	Adrian Dodson	former IBO Super Middleweight Champion
4	Audley Harrison	Olympic gold medallist and MBE
5	Jim McDonnell	former European Featherweight Champion
6	Gary Mason	former British Heavyweight Champion
7	Chris Okoh	former Commonwealth Cruiserweight Champion
8	Takaloo	former WBU Light Middleweight Champion
9	Michael Watson	former Commonwealth Middleweight Champion
10	Danny Williams	former British and Commonwealth Heavyweight Champion

10 ARSENAL-SUPPORTING
LITERARY/MEDIA FOLK

	Personality	Career
1	Melvyn Bragg	Broadcaster
2	Stephen Frears	Director
3	Brian Glanville	Sports writer, author
4	Maurice Gran	Comedy writer, scriptwriter
5	Nick Hornby	Author
6	Sir Nicholas Lloyd	Journalist
7	Laurence Marks	Comedy writer, scriptwriter
8	Piers Morgan	Journalist, author and broadcaster
9	Andrew Motion	Poet
10	Eleanor Oldroyd	Radio presenter

10 FANZINE NAMES

1   *Arsenal Echo Echo*
2   *The Arsenal Pub & Drinking Guide*
3   *Up the Arse*
4   *The Gooner*
5   *Gunflash*
6   *Highbury High*
7   *Highbury Wizard*
8   *An Imperfect Match*
9   *On the Box*
10 *One–Nil Down, Two–One Up*

10 FASHIONABLE
GUNNERS

1 **Denis Compton** was the first Brylcreem Boy.

2 **Cesc Fabregas** is already a pin-up and hopes to become a model in the future: 'I'd like that, yes – maybe one day.'

3 **Charlie George** became a role model for male fans who copied his hairstyle and shirt-out-of-shorts look.

4 **George Graham** opened a tailoring business in conjunction with Terry Venables and Ron Harris.

5 **Thierry Henry** is an international ambassador for Tommy Hilfiger.

6 **Freddie Ljungberg** has famously modelled underwear for Calvin Klein.

7 **Marc Overmars** launched a clothing range called '11' (his shirt number at Arsenal).

8 **Emmanuel Petit** ran a clothes shop in London's Sloane Street.

9 **Robert Pires** modelled for French Connection.

10 **David Seaman** was the face of Max Factor.

10 MEMORABLE
HAIRSTYLES

1   **Cesc Fabregas** had an astonishing mullet when he first joined the Club.

2   **Perry Groves** was nicknamed Tintin because of his spiky crop.

3   **Glenn Helder's** wet-look perm earned him the nickname Lionel Richie.

4   **Freddie Ljungberg** had a range of fashionable styles, most memorably the red Mohican he dyed into his mop in the 2002 Double season.

5   **Charlie Nicholas's** combination of mullet and wedge became a very popular request in north London barbershops.

6   **Emmanuel Petit** had a magnificent ponytail.

7   **Bacary Sagna's** blond dreadlocks once disappeared, then reappeared in the space of a week.

8   **David Seaman** also sported a magnificent ponytail.

9   **Alan Sunderland** had the greatest mop of curly hair ever seen at Highbury.

10   **Ian Wright** had a short period as a blond in the 1995–96 season.

10 SHIRT-NUMBER FACTS

1. The first use of shirt numbers in English football was for an Arsenal v Chelsea game in August 1928.

2. The League Cup Final of 1993 between Arsenal and Sheffield Wednesday was the first match in England in which a different number for each member of the squad was used.

3. When Tony Adams left Arsenal in 2002 there was a campaign to 'retire' the number 6 shirt as a tribute to his contribution to the Club.

4. When Dennis Bergkamp joined the Club in 1995 he asked if he could have the number 10 shirt, which was then owned by Paul Merson. Merson's reply? 'Blimey, it's Dennis Bergkamp! No problem!'

5. Number 10 became synonymous with Bergkamp, so when he retired Arsène Wenger passed the shirt number to defender William Gallas to avoid any striker suffering from comparisons with the Dutchman.

6. Theo Walcott grew up idolizing former Gunners captain Thierry Henry and later chose to take the Frenchman's number 14 shirt.

7. Number 11 has been owned by two legendary Dutchmen during Wenger's reign: Marc Overmars and Robin van Persie.

8. Number 23 was chosen by Sol Campbell as a tribute to basketball player Michael Jordan, who had the same number at the Chicago Bulls and Washington Wizards.

9. Emmanuel Adebayor chose number 25 to emulate his hero and predecessor Nwankwo Kanu, who had the same number during his Gunners years.

10. In the Premiership era the Club has regularly used squad numbers into the 30s (Traore took the number 30 in the 2008–09 season).

10 BLOND BOMBSHELLS

1   Dennis Bergkamp
2   Lee Chapman
3   Alex Cropley
4   Lee Dixon
5   Siggi Johnson
6   Alex Manninger
7   Emmanuel Petit
8   David Price
9   Stefan Schwarz
10 George Wood

FASHION

10 CURLY-HAIRED
GUNNERS

1. Paul Barron
2. Liam Brady
3. Tommy Caton
4. Gilles Grimandi
5. Jimmy Harvey
6. John Jensen
7. Brian Kidd
8. Ray Parlour
9. Graham Rix
10. Alan Sunderland

10 ARSENAL REDHEADS

1 Alan Ball
2 Perry Groves
3 John Hartson
4 Colin Hill
5 Freddie Ljungberg
6 Terry Neill
7 Ray Parlour
8 Herbert Roberts
9 Olafur-ingi Skulason
10 Willie Young

FASHION

10 BEARDED/FACIAL-HAIRED GUNNERS

1   **Ian Allinson** (moustache)

2   **Viv Anderson** (moustache)

3   **George Armstrong** (major sideburns)

4   **Brian Chambers** (moustache)

5   **John Hawley** (moustache)

6   **John Jensen** (moustache)

7   **Robert Pires** (extravagant beardage)

8   **Kevin Richardson** (moustache)

9   **David Seaman** (moustache)

10   **Alan Sunderland** (moustache)

10 FOLLICALLY CHALLENGED GUNNERS

1 Steve Bould
2 Pascal Cygan
3 George Graham (as manager)
4 Don Howe
5 Terry Mancini
6 Luis Boa Morte
7 Jock Rutherford
8 Arthur Shaw
9 Paul Shaw
10 Mikael Silvestre

"Steve Bould, Steve Bould, Stevie, Stevie Bould," sang the Arsenal fans, "He's got no hair but we don't care, Stevie, Stevie Bould." Neither should they have cared – Bould was integral in three League title-winning campaigns and the European Cup Winners Cup Final victory. Indeed this list proves that a lack of hair is no barrier to success – George Graham led Arsenal to six trophies as a manager, Pascal Cygan won a Premiership title, Luis Boa Morte did the same and Mikael Silvestre won a host of medals at Manchester United.

THE 10 LONGEST-SERVING PREMIERSHIP MANAGERS*

	Manager	Club	Length of time
1	Alex Ferguson	Manchester United	22 years 6 months
2	Arsène Wenger	Arsenal	12 years 7 months
3	David Moyes	Everton	7 years 2 months
4	Rafael Benitez	Liverpool	4 years 11 months
5	Gareth Southgate	Middlesbrough	2 years 11 months
6	Tony Pulis	Stoke City	2 years 11 months
7	Martin O'Neill	Aston Villa	2 years 9 months
8	Tony Mowbray	West Bromwich Albion	2 years 7 months
9	Phil Brown	Hull City	2 years 5 months
10	Gary Megson	Bolton Wanderers	1 year 7 months

* Correct as of end of 2008–09 season.

	Manager	Date	Club
1	Alan Ball	November 1995	Manchester City
2	George Graham	November 1997	Leeds United
3	Arsène Wenger	March 1998	Arsenal
4	Arsène Wenger	April 1998	Arsenal
5	David O'Leary	March 1999	Leeds United
6	Arsène Wenger	October 2000	Arsenal
7	David O'Leary	March 2001	Leeds United
8	David O'Leary	April 2001	Leeds United
9	Arsène Wenger	April 2002	Arsenal
10	Arsène Wenger	September 2002	Arsenal

THE 10 LONGEST MANAGERIAL REIGNS*

	Manager	Reign	Length of time
1	George Allison	June 1934–May 1947	12 years 11 months
2	Arsène Wenger	October 1996–	12 years 5 months
3	Bertie Mee	June 1966–May 1976	9 years 11 months
4	Herbert Chapman	June 1925–January 1934	8 years 7 months
5	Tom Whittaker	June 1947–October 1956	9 years 4 months
6	George Graham	June 1986–February 1995	8 years 8 months
7	Terry Neill	July 1976–December 1983	7 years 5 months
8	George Morrell	February 1908–May 1915	7 years 3 months
9	Leslie Knighton	May 1919–June 1925	6 years 1 month
10	Harry Bradshaw	August 1899–May 1904	4 years 8 months

* Correct as of the end of the 2008–09 season.

	Manager	Reign	Length of time
1	Pat Rice	September 1996	14 days
2	Stewart Houston	August 1996	1 month
3	Steve Burtenshaw	March–May 1996	2 months
4	Stewart Houston	February–June 1995	5 months
5	Joe Shaw	January–June 1934	6 months
6	Thomas Mitchell	August 1897–March 1898	8 months
7	Bruce Rioch	July 1995–August 1996	1 year 1 month
8	George Elcoat	March 1898–May 1899	1 year 2 months
9	Jack Crayston	October 1956–May 1958	1 year 8 months
10	Phil Kelso	July 1904–February 1908	3 years 7 months

10 MANAGEMENT DEBUTS

	Manager	Match and score	Date
1	Jack Crayston	Everton 4–0 Arsenal	27/10/1956
2	George Graham	Arsenal 1–0 Manchester United	23/8/1986
3	Don Howe	Arsenal 3–1 Watford	17/12/1983
4	Bertie Mee	Sunderland 1–3 Arsenal	20/8/1966
5	Terry Neill	Arsenal 0–1 Bristol City	21/8/1976
6	Bruce Rioch	Arsenal 1–1 Middlesbrough	23/8/1995
7	George Swindin	Preston North End 1–2 Arsenal	23/8/1958
8	Arsène Wenger	Blackburn Rovers 0–2 Arsenal	12/10/1996
9	Tom Whittaker	Arsenal 3–1 Sunderland	23/8/1947
10	Billy Wright	Leyton Orient 1–2 Arsenal	18/8/1962

10 NOTABLE MANAGERIAL ACHIEVEMENTS BY FORMER GUNNERS

1 Colin Addison
The striker was in charge of non-League Hereford United during their 1971–72 FA Cup run, which saw them defeat Newcastle United.

2 Dave Bowen
Not only did he steer Northampton Town from the Fourth to the First Division in the 1960s, but Bowen was also part-time manager of Wales between 1964 and 1974.

3 Tommy Docherty
He took Chelsea to League Cup victory when they beat Leicester City in the 1965 Final and also led Manchester United to the 1976 FA Cup Final, where they finished runners-up to Southampton.

4 Bobby Gould
He was at the helm as Wimbledon pulled off one of the most famous FA Cup upsets of all time, beating Liverpool in the 1988 Final at Wembley.

5 George Graham
As manager of Tottenham Hotspur he led the club to the 1999 League Cup Final, where they beat Leicester City 1–0.

6 David Halliday
During his 18-year reign at Aberdeen, the club won a League title, a Scottish FA Cup and a League Cup.

7 **Brian Kidd**

As manager of Manchester United's youth team he was influential in Ryan Giggs's development. He was then promoted to assistant manager and helped guide the club through a glorious period that included two Doubles.

8 **Joe Mercer**

As well as winning cups as manager of Aston Villa and Manchester City, he was the caretaker manager of England for seven matches after the resignation of Sir Alf Ramsey.

9 **David O'Leary**

He took Leeds United to the semi-finals of the UEFA Champions League in 2001.

10 **Brian Talbot**

He led the Maltese side Hibernians to two successive Premier League championships in the 1990s (1993 and 1994).

	Chairman	Date
1	Peter Hill-Wood	1982–
2	Denis Hill-Wood	1962–82
3	Sir Bracewell Smith	1949–62
4	Sir Samuel Hill-Wood	1946–49
5	Viscount Castlereagh	1939–46
6	8th Earl of Granard	1936–39
7	5th Earl of Lonsdale	1936
8	Sir Samuel Hill-Wood	1929–36
9	Sir Henry Norris	1912–29
10	George Leavey	1912

THE 10 HIGHEST MANAGERS' POINTS TALLIES*

	Manager	Points
1	Arsène Wenger	996
2	George Graham	576
3	Bertie Mee	477
4	Tom Whittaker	458
5	Herbert Chapman	432
6	Terry Neill	397
7	George Allison	295
8	George Morrell	255
9	Leslie Knighton	231
10	George Swindin	173

* Up until the end of the 2008–09 season.

Three points for a win was introduced to English football in 1981, giving Arsène Wenger, George Graham and Terry Neill an advantage in this list.

10 HONOURS AWARDED
TO MANAGERS

	Manager	Honour	Date
1	Herbert Chapman	Inducted into the English Football Hall of Fame	2003
2	Herbert Chapman	Voted greatest British manager of all time by the *Sunday Times*	2004
3	Herbert Chapman	English Heritage blue plaque outside his house in Hendon	2005
4	Bertie Mee	OBE	1984
5	Arsène Wenger	Légion d'Honneur	2002
6	Arsène Wenger	OBE	2003
7	Arsène Wenger	Freedom of the Borough of Islington	2004
8	Arsène Wenger	Inducted into the English Football Hall of Fame	2006
9	Arsène Wenger	Arsenal-supporting astronomer Ian P. Griffin names asteroid '33179 Arsènewenger' after him	1998
10	Tom Whittaker	MBE	1945

HERBERT CHAPMAN'S FIRST 10 CLUBS AS A PLAYER

	Club	Played
1	Ashton North End	1895–97
2	Stalybridge Rovers	1897
3	Rochdale	1897–98
4	Grimsby Town	1898–99
5	Swindon Town	1899
6	Sheppey United	1899–1900
7	Worksop Town	1900–01
8	Northampton Town	1901–02
9	Sheffield United	1902–03
10	Notts County	1903–05

10 HERBERT CHAPMAN
INNOVATIONS

1 FA Cup side by side
For the FA Cup Final of 1930, the players of Arsenal and Huddersfield Town emerged from the tunnel side by side. This was at Chapman's suggestion and has been followed ever since.

2 Clapping all four sides of the ground
He instructed the players to clap all four sides of the ground as a mark of respect to supporters.

3 Tube station
On 5 November 1932 the local Gillespie Road tube station was renamed 'Arsenal' after pressure from Chapman. Thousands of tickets, maps and signs had to be replaced. The Club remains the only one in London to have a tube station named after it.

4 Numbered shirts
He introduced numbered shirts to the game during the 1920s. The earliest record of them being worn is on 25 August 1928, when Arsenal played away at Sheffield Wednesday.

5 Shirt styles
During the 1932–33 season Chapman noticed a fan wearing a red sleeveless jumper over a white shirt and decided that this combination of colours would help the players identify each other more easily on the pitch than the existing all-red shirts. The new-look shirt was introduced in March 1933 and the Gunners won the title that season. Two years later he introduced hoops on the players' socks, again to aid identification.

6 White balls

He noticed that a brown ball being kicked around a muddy pitch was hard for both players and spectators to see. He therefore introduced white balls to make the game easier to follow.

7 Formations

Prior to 1925 most teams played a 2-3-5 formation. However, after the offside law was changed that year, Chapman introduced a 3-2-2-3 formation, a more attacking unit that ushered in a golden era of success.

8 Floodlights

He had a 'light-bulb moment' in the 1930s, realizing that floodlights could be used at football grounds. They were installed at Highbury in 1932, though the authorities would not sanction their use for competitive games until the 1950s.

9 Semicircle

The semicircle that you see on the edge of the penalty box was first suggested by Chapman.

10 European travel

He took the Gunners to the Continent for friendly games and tours, making the players famous across western Europe long before official European competitions were thought of.

1   In 1998 Arsenal became one of the first clubs to be awarded Academy status.

2   Wenger played a key role in planning the Emirates Stadium, including the size of the pitch and the design and temperature of the dressing rooms.

3   He revolutionized the diet and nutritional intake of the team, making innovations that have since been replicated by other clubs.

4   He arranged for the temperature on the team bus to be raised in order to keep the players' muscles supple.

5   He was also closely involved with the design of the new Training Centre, even selecting the furniture and cutlery.

6   He increased the amount of stretching players did and employed masseurs.

7   He and his stopwatch made training an increasingly regimented affair, with each segment timed to the second.

8   He began the tradition of sending players with troublesome injuries for treatment in the South of France. Witness the miraculous effect this had on Robert Pires and Tony Adams.

9   He offered a replay in the 1998–99 FA Cup after the Gunners beat Sheffield United by a controversial goal at Highbury.

10 His success prompted the Club to commission a bronze bust of him, making Wenger the first manager to be so honoured since that other great innovator, Herbert Chapman.

	Manager	Date	%
1	Arsène Wenger	1996–	64.36
2	Thomas Mitchell	1897–98	53.85
3	George Elcoat	1898–99	53.49
4	Harry Bradshaw	1899–1904	50.79
5	Herbert Chapman	1925–34	49.88
6	George Graham	1986–95	48.91
7	Don Howe	1983–86	48.28
8	Tom Whittaker	1947–56	47.20
9	Bruce Rioch	1995–96	46.81
10	George Allison	1934–47	46.29

* Source: *The Official Arsenal Factfile*. Correct as of end of season 2008–09.

	Manager	Wins
1	Arsène Wenger	134
2	Bertie Mee	119
3	Tom Whittaker	116
4	Herbert Chapman	109
5	George Graham	95
6	Terry Neill	85
7	George Allison	72
8	Leslie Knighton	63
9	George Swindin	44
10	Billy Wright	40

THE 10 HIGHEST-SELLING ARSENAL FC PRODUCTS ON WWW.AMAZON.CO.UK*

1 Arsenal FC: Duvet Cover Set (single)

2 *The Official Arsenal Annual*

3 *The Official Arsenal Illustrated History 1886–2008*

4 *Arsenal: Extraordinary Images of an Extraordinary Club*

5 *Arsenal: The Official Biography – The Compelling Story of an Amazing Club*

6 Official Arsenal Football Club Calendar 2009

7 Official Arsenal Wall Calendar 2009

8 *The Official Arsenal Illustrated History 1886–2007*

9 The Official Arsenal Slim Diary

10 *Arsenal: 49 – The Complete Unbeaten Record* (DVD)

* In February 2009.

	Item	Price
1	Arsenal FC hand-signed players team mount	£89.99
2	Arsenal FC stadium 'Legends' tour: gift voucher for 2	£85.00
3	Fabregas Arsenal FC canvas art print poster (large)	£79.99
4	Arsenal FC stadium 'Legends' tour: gift voucher	£70.00
5	Men's Nike Arsenal FC Fly Emirates tracksuit (red)	£59.99
6	Fabregas Arsenal FC canvas art print poster (large)	£49.99
7	Arsenal FC official framed 'colours' print picture	£44.99
8	Arsenal FC newspaper archive book	£43.99
9	Arsenal FC signed photo – Rosicky/RVP/Adebayor/Fabregas	£39.99
10	Tony Adams Arsenal FC pop art canvas print (A1)	£34.95

* In February 2009.

10 NUMBER ONE HITS ON THE DAY PLAYERS WERE BORN

	Player	Date of birth	Song
1	Emmanuel Adebayor	26/2/1984	*99 Red Balloons* (Nena)
2	Manuel Almunia	17/5/1977	*I Don't Want to Talk About It* (Rod Stewart)
3	Andrei Arshavin	29/5/1981	*Stand and Deliver* (Adam and the Ants)
4	Nicklas Bendtner	16/1/1988	*Heaven is a Place on Earth* (Belinda Carlisle)
5	Gael Clichy	26/7/1985	*There Must Be an Angel (Playing with My Heart)* (The Eurythmics)
6	Samir Nasri	26/7/1987	*Star Trekkin'* (The Firm)
7	Robin van Persie	6/8/1983	*Wherever I Lay My Hat (That's My Home)* (Paul Young)
8	Bacary Sagna	14/2/1983	*Too Shy* (Kajagoogoo)
9	Kolo Toure	19/3/1981	*Jealous Guy* (Roxy Music)
10	Theo Walcott	16/3/1989	*Too Many Broken Hearts* (Jason Donovan)

10 PRE-MATCH TUNES
PLAYED AT HOME GAMES

1. **Anchors Aweigh,** Metropolitan Police Band led by Constable Alex Morgan: a regular part of the pre-match entertainment at Highbury in the 1970s.

2. **The Champions League Anthem,** an adaptation by Tony Britten of Handel's *Zadok the Priest*: played before every UEFA Champions League tie.

3. **Good Old Arsenal,** 1971 Arsenal FC FA Cup squad: regularly played before home matches at Highbury.

4. **Good Old Arsenal,** remix by Shovell and Charlie George: regularly played before home matches at Highbury and the Emirates.

5. **Hot Stuff,** 1998 Arsenal FC FA Cup squad: regularly played before home matches at Highbury.

6. **Premier League 'handshake music'***

7. **Right Here, Right Now,** Fatboy Slim: regularly played before home matches at Highbury and the Emirates.

8. **Simply the Best,** Tina Turner: regularly played before home matches at Highbury in the mid-1990s.

9. **Theme from the A Team,** Mike Post and Pete Carpenter: the team took to the field to this song at Highbury in the 1980s.

10. **The Wonder of You,** Elvis Presley: the team took to the field to this song at the Emirates in the 2007–08 season.

* Played as the two teams shake hands prior to the kick-off.

1   *Born to Run* (Bruce Springsteen) Theo Walcott – so quick he could trigger speed cameras out jogging.

2   *Hold the Line* (Toto) Tony Adams – no one organized the back line and offside trap better.

3   *Leader of the Pack* (The Shangri-Las) Patrick Vieira – a great warrior and captain.

4   *Nothing Compares 2 U* (Sinead O'Connor) Thierry Henry – incomparable and untouchable in his striking pomp.

5   *Respect* (Aretha Franklin) Dennis Bergkamp – grace on and off the pitch.

6   *Rock Around the Clock* (Bill Haley and His Comets) the Arsenal fans – Highbury is gone but the clock ticks on.

7   *Simply the Best* (Tina Turner) Cesc Fabregas – pure class in possession.

8   *Teenage Kicks* (The Undertones) Jack Wilshere – young, gifted and ready to come of age.

9   *This Charming Man* (The Smiths) Arsène Wenger – Intelligent and polite, a true gentleman in a sport short of them.

10 *Unbelievable* (EMF) Ian Wright – goals and glory, time after time.

* Henry Winter is the *Daily Telegraph*'s Football Correspondent.

10 MEMORABLE HEADLINES

1   **'Arsenal win the World Cup', *Daily Mirror*, 13/7/1998**
    When France beat Brazil in the World Cup Final, thanks in part to an
    Emmanuel Petit goal set up by Patrick Vieira, Gunners fan Piers
    Morgan emblazoned the front page of the newspaper he edited with
    this unforgettable headline.

2   **'Arsène Who?', *Evening Standard*, 20/8/1996**
    The appointment of Arsène Wenger in 1996 surprised many
    observers, not least the headline writers of London's evening paper.

3   **'Lewin some, you lose some', *Official Arsenal Magazine*,
    June 2005**
    The Club magazine has come up with some memorable pun-based
    headlines for its interviews with Gunners greats. This one introduced
    their interview with former Club physio Gary Lewin.

4   **'You don't have a prayer, Arsenal', *Daily Mail*, 26/5/1989**
    When the team learned of this headline en route to their title-
    deciding clash at Anfield, Paul Merson quipped, 'Let us pray.'
    Arsenal went on to win 2–0 and lift the League title.

5   **'Polar Gunner Solo Skier', *Official Arsenal Magazine*,
    July 2005**
    Another classic from the Club magazine, this introduced its interview
    with Erling Kagge, who is a Norwegian Everest climber and solo
    North and South Pole skier.

6 'After 98 games, two years, four months, two weeks, two days, one hour and 19 minutes – Jensen scores!', *News of the World*, 1/1/1995

When the wait for John Jensen's first Arsenal goal finally came to an end the Gunners fans went wild. So too did the headline writers!

7 'Absolutely Fabregas', *Daily Mirror*, 29/3/2006

After Arsenal beat Juventus 2–0 in the quarter-final of the UEFA Champions League, the *Mirror* paid tribute to the contribution of rising star Cesc Fabregas.

8 'Unbeaten Arsenal in football heaven', *Observer*, 16/5/2004

The press went to town when Arsenal ended the 2003–04 season as unbeaten champions. The broadsheet captured the mood perfectly.

9 'Made It', *Daily Mirror*, 1/5/1980

It took four games to separate Arsenal and Liverpool in the FA Cup semi-final. The *Mirror* summed up the joy of Gunners fans when Brian Talbot's winner sent the Club to the Final.

10 'Nil–Nil to the Arsenal', *Daily Mirror*, 8/3/2006

Having already gone one goal ahead in the first leg, Arsenal were delighted to draw 0–0 in the second leg against Real Madrid. This headline conveyed the fact that the draw was effectively a victory.

1 *The Arsenal Stadium Mystery*, **1939** A murder-mystery flick set in Highbury.

2 *Frenzy*, **1972** A pub featured in this Alfred Hitchcock thriller has an Arsenal stained-glass window.

3 *Lamb*, **1985** Part of this film was filmed on the North Bank at Highbury.

4 *The Young Americans*, **1993** This gangster movie includes footage of an Arsenal game.

5 *When Saturday Comes*, **1996** A Sheffield United v Arsenal match sees star Sean Bean make a substitute appearance.

6 *Fever Pitch*, **1997** The dramatization of Nick Hornby's bestselling book about his love of Arsenal.

7 *The Full Monty*, **1997** The Adams/Bould/Dixon/Winterburn back four is name-checked in this feel-good flick.

8 *Plunkett and Macleane*, **1999** This dandy highwayman movie features two characters called Winterburn and Dixon.

9 *The Baby Juice Express*, **2001** David Seaman and Ray Parlour made brief appearances.

10 *About a Boy*, **2002** In another dramatization of a Hornby book, an Arsenal flag can be spotted by eagle-eyed viewers.

THE 10 2008–09 SQUAD MEMBERS WITH MOST GOOGLE HITS*

	Player	Hits
1	Cesc Fabregas	2,110,000
2	Robin van Persie	1,070,000
3	Samir Nasri	893,000
4	Emmanuel Adebayor	888,000
5	Theo Walcott	858,000
6	William Gallas	844,000
7	Andrey Arshavin	678,000
8	Kolo Toure	670,000
9	Tomas Rosicky	492,000
10	Manuel Almunia	350,000

* Figures correct as of January 2009.

THE 10 2008–09 SQUAD MEMBERS WITH MOST FANS ON FACEBOOK*

	Player	Fans
1	Cesc Fabregas	59,288
2	Andrey Arshavin	58,194
3	Samir Nasri	48,202
4	Theo Walcott	32,020
5	Robin van Persie	26,222
6	Aaron Ramsey	8,905
7	Gael Clichy	7,663
8	William Gallas	5,900
9	Jack Wilshere	5,000
10	Emmanuel Adebayor	4,874

* From each player's (unauthorized) Facebook page. Figures correct as of January 2009.

10 QUIRKY FAN GROUP NAMES ON FACEBOOK

1   Block 4 Row 1 & 2 Emirates Stadium

2   Cesc Fabregas Rocks!!!!!!!!!!!!!!!!!!!

3   'Champagne' Charlie Nicholas Makes *Soccer Saturday*

4   Charlie George Disciples

5   Clap for Arsène Wenger

6   Robin van Persie is da Best

7   Shovell – Next Arsenal Manager

8   The I Love Theo Walcott More Than is Probably Legal Fan Club

9   Tony Adams is God

10 Would Love to Meet Ian Wright

	Player	Results
1	William Gallas	50
2	Cesc Fabregas	43
3	Theo Walcott	24
4	Robin van Persie	19
5	Tomas Rosicky	10
6	Emmanuel Adebayor	9
7	Samir Nasri	8
8	Kolo Toure	6
9	Mikael Silvestre	4
10	Gael Clichy	2

* Figures correct as of February 2009.

10 SONGS
ABOUT ARSENAL

1   *Arsenal We All Love You*, Arsenal Choir, 2002

2   *Bob Wilson: Anchor Man*, Half Man Half Biscuit, 2001

3   *Highbury Sunshine*, Yeah, 2001

4   *I Wish I Could Play Like Charlie George*, The Strikers and Selston Bagthorpe Primary School Choir, 2002

5   *Ooh Ooh Tony Adams*, The A Team, 1995

6   *Sol's a Gooner*, The Viera Boys, 2002

7   *The Gus Caesar Rap*, Stephen North and the Flat Back Four, 1995

8   *The Only Cockney Rebel (That Meant Anything to Me was Charlie George)*, The Half Time Oranges, 1998

9   *The Victory Song*, Enrico Cocozza, 1993

10 *Thiery Henry*, Arsène Sings, 2001

10 MEMORABLE COMMENTARY LINES

1   'And Arsenal come streaming forward in what will surely be their last attack. A good ball by Dixon, finding Smith, to Thomas, charging through the midfield. It's up for grabs now'
Brian Moore, Liverpool 0–2 Arsenal, 26 May 1989

2   'Oh, Brady won it beautifully, look at that! Oh, look at that! What a goal by Brady. A marvellous goal designed for the big occasion'
John Motson, Tottenham Hotspur 0–5 Arsenal, 23 December 1978

3   'And it's Adam, put through by Bould – would you believe it? That sums it all up'
Martin Tyler, Arsenal 4–0 Everton, 3 May 1998

4   'It's Ian Wright, so good they named him thrice: Ian Wright, Wright, Wright'
Jonathan Pearce, Arsenal 3–0 Standard Liège, 20 October 1993

5   'The Championship, and a place among history, goes to Arsenal'
Martin Tyler, Arsenal 2–1 Leicester City, 15 May 2004

6   'Oh no, he's got through. Oh, it's all right, it's only Ray Parlour'
Tim Lovejoy, Arsenal 2–0 Chelsea, 4 May 2002

7 'Handy Andy Linighan. The boy from Hartlepool is in the big pool of London football, and he's become the biggest fish of them all'
Jonathan Pearce, Arsenal 2–1 Sheffield Wednesday, 20 May 1993

8 'Kannnnnnuuuuu. That is AMAZING'
Barry Davies, Chelsea 2–3 Arsenal, 23 October 1999

9 'And Arsenal finally lose their unbeaten record after drawing with Liverpool'
unnamed Fox Sports commentator, Arsenal 1–1 Liverpool, 28 October 2007

10 'As a neutral, I'm desperate for Arsenal to score a third'
Andy Gray, Aston Villa 2–2 Arsenal, 26 December 2008

THE 10 MOST POPULAR EPISODES OF THE OFFICIAL ARSENAL PODCAST*

	Downloads	Date	Game
1	6,412	29/8/2008	Newcastle United (h)
2	5,573	15/8/2008	West Bromwich Albion (h)
3	5,489	3/10/2008	Sunderland (a)
4	5,100	22/10/2008	Fulham (a)
5	4,878	12/9/2008	Blackburn Rovers (a)
6	4,516	19/9/2008	Bolton Wanderers (a)
7	4,328	26/9/2008	Hull City (h)
8	4,203	23/9/2008	Sheffield United (h)
9	4,000	7/11/2008	Manchester United (h)
10	3,934	30/9/2008	Porto (h)

* Podcasts go live the day before each game, with the exceptions of Cup games, which go live on the day of the game.

10 TV PUNDITS

1   **Liam Brady** is a regular on Irish television, making astute observations on Champions League and Premiership games.

2   **Lee Dixon** appears on both *Football Focus* and *Match of the Day* on the BBC.

3   **Martin Keown** often performs alongside Lee Dixon on *Football Focus*.

4   **Frank McLintock** is virtually an institution on Sky Sports, featuring regularly on *Gillette Soccer Saturday*.

5   **Bob McNab** was part of ITV's commentary team for the 1970 World Cup.

6   **Charlie Nicholas** is a regular on Sky Sports' *Gillette Soccer Saturday* and *Monday Night Football*.

8   **Fay White** has appeared on Sky Sports, Eurosport and the BBC's *Football Focus* and *Match of the Day 2*, among others.

9   **Bob Wilson** spent 28 years on a range of shows, including the BBC's *Grandstand* and *Match of the Day* and ITV's Champions League coverage.

10 **Ian Wright** has presented his own chat show on ITV, been a regular on the BBC's *Match of the Day* and now co-presents a show on TalkSport radio.

10 MUSICAL AND DANCING GUNNERS

1 **Tony Adams** learned to play the piano in the late 1990s and started going to opera performances.

2 **Julio Baptista** was filmed playing the ukulele on YouTube.

3 **Kevin Campbell** set up his own record label called 2 Wikid.

4 **Lee Dixon** has taken drum lessons.

5 **Charlie George** recorded a song, under the name Charlie Gorgeous, called *A Love Song for My Lady*.

6 **Gilberto** was filmed playing the guitar on YouTube.

7 **Gilles Grimandi** plays the piano.

8 **Peter Marinello,** a big music fan, was once a studio guest on *Top of the Pops*.

9 **David Seaman** won the one-off special *Strictly Ice Dancing*, a spin-off from *Strictly Come Dancing*, before appearing on the series *Dancing on Ice*.

10 **Ian Wright** released a song entitled *Do the Wright Thing*.

10 AUTOBIOGRAPHY TITLES

	Title	Author
1	*Allison Calling*	George Allison
2	*Football Ambassador*	Eddie Hapgood
3	*Footballeur*	Robert Pires
4	*Revelations of a Football Manager*	Terry Neill
5	*Rockbottom*	Paul Merson
6	*So Far So Good*	Liam Brady
7	*Tappy*	Derek Tapscott
8	*True Grit*	Frank McLintock
9	*We All Live in a Perry Groves World*	Perry Groves
10	*You've Got to Be Crazy*	Bob Wilson

1 **Arsenal 2–1 Southampton, 26/3/1927**
This match, played at a wet and windy Stamford Bridge, was
Arsenal's first win in an FA Cup semi-final.

2 **Southampton 0–4 Arsenal, 28/9/1991**
Ian Wright scored his first League goal in this match at the Dell.
Indeed, he scored a hat-trick...

3 **Arsenal 5–1 Southampton, 2/5/1992**
... as he did in the final game of the same season. These goals
confirmed him as winner of the Golden Boot and were the final
strikes in front of a standing North Bank.

4 **Arsenal 4–2 Southampton, 23/9/1995**
Having waited weeks for the first Dennis Bergkamp goal, two came
along in the same game as the Dutchman broke his duck in this tie.

5 **Southampton 1–3 Arsenal, 23/8/1997**
Just as Dennis Bergkamp broke his duck against the Saints, so did
fellow Dutchman Marc Overmars.

6 **Southampton 0–1 Arsenal, 18/9/1999**
So too did Thierry Henry, in the final match Arsenal played at
the Dell.

7   **Arsenal 6–1 Southampton, 7/5/2003**
As well as featuring a pair of hat-tricks by Gunners whose surnames
begin with 'P' (Robert Pires and Jermaine Pennant), this was also the
start of the 49-match unbeaten League run.

8   **Arsenal 1–0 Southampton, 17/5/2003**
This was the first FA Cup Final played under cover and saw the
Gunners triumph.

9   **Arsenal 2–2 Southampton, 30/10/2005**
Having begun the 49-match unbeaten League run at home against
Southampton, the Gunners' first match after losing at Old Trafford
was at home against the Saints.

10   **Arsenal 2–2 Southampton, 30/10/2005**
Robin van Persie scored the equalizer in the same game – his first
goal from a free-kick for the Club.

10 CURIOUS ITEMS IN THE ARSENAL MUSEUM*

1 Souvenir cricket match programme

Arsenal FC and Middlesex County Cricket Club have had a close association since the Compton brothers, Denis and Leslie, played for both before and after World War II. A souvenir programme shows that on 12/8/1949 a cricket match was played between the two clubs at Highbury for Denis Compton's testimonial.

2 Promotional material from the World Heavyweight Boxing Championship

On 21/5/1966 Henry Cooper challenged Muhammad Ali for the World Heavyweight Championship at Highbury. A crowd of 45,000 saw the fight stopped when Cooper sustained a badly cut eye. He was invited to the last match ever played at Highbury.

3 Golfing memorabilia

Arsenal's legendary manager Herbert Chapman said of his players, 'Get them out golfing and they will forget their problems.' A regular players' golf tournament was organized and memorabilia on display includes Wilf Copping's bag and clubs from the 1930s and the tournament trophy won by full back Len Wills in 1960.

4 Material from *The Arsenal Stadium Mystery*

In 1939 Arsenal players and management appeared in this major British feature film, which tells the story of a player murdered while playing at Highbury.

5 Ceremonial chair from a Yorkshire church

Herbert Chapman was a religious man and, after his death in 1934, his church in Yorkshire presented Arsenal with his chair. For many years it was located in the boardroom at Highbury.

6 Single horseshoe

When Highbury was being constructed in 1913 it was rumoured that a horse and cart fell into a deep hole on the North Bank, the horse was killed and both horse and cart were buried there. In 2006, when the stadium was demolished, a single horseshoe was discovered.

7 19th century cannonball

Arsenal FC was formed by a group of workers at the Royal Arsenal munitions factory in Woolwich in 1886, the nickname 'The Gunners' reflecting that historical connection. The cannonball in the museum was produced in a foundry at the munitions factory.

8 Cigarette box from 1893

On display is a silver cigarette box decorated with a photograph of the first professional Arsenal team of 1893. It carries the inscription 'Presented to Lieutenant W. Simpson from a few football friends as a mark of their esteem. May 1893'.

9 Rectangular piece of turf

This is no ordinary piece of grass. It is the centre circle from Highbury, preserved as a lasting reminder of the pitch on which so many great football matches were played over 93 years.

10 Statue of Romulus and Remus

It is traditional that clubs in the Champions League present their opponents with a gift before the match. In 2002 Arsenal played Roma and they presented Arsenal with this statue of Romulus and Remus being suckled by the she-wolf.

* As compiled by Anthony Sandell, Arsenal Museum tour guide.

WHAT 10 PLAYERS WOULD TAKE TO A DESERT ISLAND

	Player	Item
1	Manuel Almunia	'My wife'
2	Amaury Bischoff	'Am I allowed to take my family?'
3	Gael Clichy	'A football'
4	Denilson	'My mobile phone'
5	Emmanuel Eboue	'My wife'
6	Johan Djourou	'My brother'
7	Justin Hoyte	'My girlfriend'
8	Vito Mannone	'Luxury food'
9	Tomas Rosicky	'My mobile phone'
10	Bacary Sagna	'My family'

10 LOOKALIKES

1. **Tony Adams** and **Nicholas Lyndhurst** (Rodney in *Only Fools and Horses*). The captain's team-mates nicknamed him 'Rodders' after Lyndhurst's most celebrated character.

2. **Adrian Clarke** and **Dean Gaffney** (Robbie Jackson in *EastEnders*). 'Go on, Robbie,' cried the fans when the young winger went on one of his runs.

3. **Cesc Fabregas** and **Gabriel Gray** (Sylar from the hit TV show *Heroes*). The Spaniard is certainly a hero to Gunners fans.

4. **Perry Groves** and **Tintin**. The winger's spiky hair made him look just like the cartoon hero in the eyes of some.

5. **Glenn Helder** and **Lionel Richie**. The fans christened the Dutchman 'Richie' because of his flowing, wet-look curls.

6. **John Jensen** and **Harry Enfield's Scousers**. 'Calm down, calm down!'

7. **Emmanuel Petit** and **Boris Becker**. The Frenchman was once asked for his autograph in Monaco and gladly signed. The grateful recipient said, 'Thanks, Mr Becker!'.

8. **Tomas Rosicky** and **Mark Owen** (Take That). Could Tomas be magic now? Yes he could.

9. **Theo Walcott** and **Lewis Hamilton** (Formula One). Walcott's team-mates have often commented on the likeness between the fast winger and the fast driver.

10. **Ian Wright** and **Luis Boa Morte**. When Portuguese forward Boa Morte first signed for the Gunners, the pair posed together and laughed at their similarity.

10 ARSENAL ANIMALS

1 The Highbury squirrel
During Arsenal's UEFA Champions League clash with Villarreal in April 2006, a squirrel ran on to the Highbury turf. In no mood to leave the pitch in a hurry, it demonstrated some deft moves before scuttling off.

2 The North Bank horse
Football legend has it that when the stand was being built, a horse fell into a large hole on the North Bank, could not be saved and was buried there. However, when the stand was rebuilt in 1992, no bones were found (see page 155 for more details).

3 Theo Walcott's dogs
Theo is just one Gunner to own pets. His dogs are called Gypsy and Diesel.

4 Fabby the cat
Gunners fans Mandy and Lucy Covey named their pet cat after Cesc Fabregas. He sometimes uses Lucy's Arsenal scarf as a bed.

5 Gilberto the anteater
Born in London Zoo in June 2003, this animal – native to Brazil – was named after the Brazilian midfield ace.

6 Plattypuss
David Platt is just one Gunner to have been given an animal nickname.

7 George Wood's birds
Goalkeeper Wood is a passionate ornithologist and describes his most memorable experience as the day he spotted a sedge warbler in Douglas Water, Lanarkshire.

8 Willie Young's kennels
The Scottish centre back now runs kennels in Bottesford, Leicestershire.

9 Pied wagtails
The Emirates Stadium has been engulfed by these birds during evening matches in the winter.

10 The Lagos cow
Arsenal supporters in Lagos, Nigeria, painted a cow in the colours of Barcelona and promptly slaughtered it at the opening whistle of the 2006 UEFA Champions League final between Arsenal and the Nou Camp giants.

10 PLAYERS WHO HAD TWO SEPARATE ARSENAL CAREERS

1 Ted Bateup, 1905–08 and 1910–11
After three years with Woolwich Arsenal, Bateup left for New Brompton. He returned two years later.

2 Frank Boulton, 1936–38 and 1940–41
The goalkeeper replaced George Swindin and won a League Championship medal in 1938, but he was then ousted by a rejuvenated Swindin and moved to Derby County. He returned to the Club during World War II and made ten appearances as a guest player.

3 Charles Buchan, 1908 and 1925–28
Having fallen out with the Club over expenses after just four games, Buchan moved to Northfleet. He returned 17 years later and became Club captain.

4 Jack Caldwell, 1894–96 and 1896–98
The Scottish left back missed just one game in his first two seasons with the Club. When he lost his place, he moved to Lanark in August 1896, but he returned the same year and resumed his Club career.

5 Hugh Duff, 1896–97 and 1898–99
Having scored on his FA Cup debut for Woolwich Arsenal, he signed for Millwall in August 1898, but he returned 11 months later.

LEFT FIELD

6   John Graham, 1898 and 1899–1900
His first stay with the Club was just four months long. He then spent two years at Millwall before returning. He made only one appearance during both spells.

7   Fred Groves, 1912–19 and 1919–21
Quite a yo-yo career for Groves. After seven years with Woolwich Arsenal he signed for Brighton and Hove Albion for £500. However, five months later he was back at Arsenal, where he stayed for two years before returning to Brighton.

8   Martin Keown, 1984–86 and 1993–2004
Having joined the Club as a schoolboy, Keown left following a disagreement over wages. After spells with Aston Villa and Everton, he returned and became a key figure during a golden era for Arsenal.

9   John Lukic, 1983–90 and 1996–2000
The goalkeeper joined Arsenal from Leeds United, then returned to Elland Road seven years later. He came back to Arsenal after six years in Yorkshire.

10   John Peart, 1910–14 and 1919–21
Peart's two Arsenal careers were interrupted by a spell with Croydon Common and four years in the army.

1   Liam Brady

2   Ashley Cole

3   George Eastham

4   Edu

5   Remi Garde

6   Robin van Persie

7   Emmanuel Petit

8   Jose Antonio Reyes

9   Silvinho

10   Nigel Winterburn

Nigel Winterburn was famed as a one-footed player, but his most memorable and important goal for the Club was delivered by his right leg. On 17/5/1989, with the Gunners chasing the League Championship, the left-back's former team Wimbledon were beating Arsenal 2–1 until a long-range, right-footed volley from Winterburn earned a vital draw.

10 CURIOUS PRE- AND POST-FOOTBALL JOBS

	Player	Job
1	Gavin Crawford	Groundsman at Charlton Athletic
2	Bertram Freeman	Silversmith
3	Thomas Graham	Ferryman
4	Albert Gudmundsson	Icelandic Minister of Finance
5	Eddie Hapgood	Youth Hostel warden
6	Sidney Hoar	Straw hat maker
7	Archie Macaulay	Traffic warden
8	Arthur Milton	Postman
9	Rami Shaaban	Mountain explosives specialist
10	Ian Ure	Prison social worker

10 BROTHERS WHO BOTH PLAYED FOR ARSENAL*

1 **Michael** (1992–99) and **Tommy** (1995–2000) **Black**
2 **William** (1900–04) and **Joseph** (1901–04) **Bradshaw**
3 **Robert** (1891–94) and **George** (1896–97) **Buist**
4 **Danny** (1953–62) and **Denis** (1957–61) **Clapton**
5 **Leslie** (1931–52) and **Denis** (1932–50) **Compton**
6 **Stefan** (1996–97) and **Valur** (1996–98) **Gislason**
7 **David** (1904–12) and **Andrew** (1908–09) **Neave**
8 **Willis** (1910–11) and **Thomas** (1911) **Rippon**
9 **Charles** (1904–10) and **Joe** (1906–08) **Satterthwaite**
10 **Kolo** (2002–) and **Yaya** (2005) **Toure**

* Kolo Toure's younger brother Yaya had a trial in the summer of 2005 and appeared in a pre-season friendly, but he did not complete a permanent move to the Club.

THE 10 BEST FA CUP
HOME WINS

	Match and score	Date
1	Arsenal 12–0 Ashford United	14/10/1893
2	Arsenal 11–0 Lyndhurst	5/10/1889
3	Arsenal 11–1 Darwen	9/1/1932
4	Arsenal 10–1 City Ramblers	29/10/1892
5	Arsenal 9–0 St Albans	30/10/1897
6	Arsenal 7–0 Crystal Palace	27/1/1934
7	Arsenal 7–2 Hereford United	22/1/1985
8	Arsenal 6–1 Plymouth Argyle	31/1/1987
9=	Arsenal 6–2 Clapton	4/11/1952
=	Arsenal 6–2 Bury	31/1/1953

	Match and score	Date
1	Burnley 1–7 Arsenal	20/2/1937
2	QPR 0–6 Arsenal	27/1/2001
3=	Norwich City 0–5 Arsenal	12/1/1952
=	Sheffield United 0–5 Arsenal	7/1/1978
5=	Small Heath 1–5 Arsenal	16/1/1892
=	Bristol Rovers 1–5 Arsenal	11/1/1936
=	Chesterfield 1–5 Arsenal	16/1/1937
=	Farnborough Town 1–5 Arsenal	25/1/2003
=	Portsmouth 1–5 Arsenal	6/3/2004
10=	Carlisle United 1–4 Arsenal	11/1/1951
=	Leeds United 1–4 Arsenal	4/1/2004

10 FA CUP FINAL
VICTORIES

	Match and score	Date
1	Arsenal 2–0 Huddersfield Town	26/4/1930
2	Arsenal 1–0 Sheffield United	25/4/1936
3	Arsenal 2–0 Liverpool	29/4/1950
4	Arsenal 2–1 Liverpool (aet)	8/5/1971
5	Arsenal 3–2 Manchester United	12/5/1979
6	Arsenal 2–1 Sheffield Wednesday (aet)	20/5/1993
7	Arsenal 2–0 Newcastle United	15/5/1998
8	Arsenal 2–0 Chelsea	4/5/2002
9	Arsenal 1–0 Southampton	17/5/2003
10	Arsenal 0–0 Manchester United (Arsenal won 5–4 on penalties)	21/5/2005

THE 10 WORST
FA CUP LOSSES AWAY

	Match and score	Date
1=	Sunderland 6–0 Arsenal	21/1/1893
=	West Ham United 6–0 Arsenal	5/1/1946
3	Burnley 6–1 Arsenal	1/2/1896
4	Everton 5–0 Arsenal	5/2/1910
5	Small Heath 5–1 Arsenal	16/1/1892
6	Manchester United 4–0 Arsenal	16/2/2008
7=	Hull City 4–1 Arsenal	16/1/1908
=	Middlesbrough 4–1 Arsenal	26/2/1977
9=	Luton Town 3–0 Arsenal	3/3/1986
=	Sheffield United 3–0 Arsenal	18/2/1959
=	Blackburn Rovers 3–0 Arsenal	22/1/1966
=	Wolverhampton Wanderers 3–0 Arsenal	3/1/1976

10 CUP SHOCKS

1   **QPR 2–0 Arsenal, FA Cup third round, 1921** The Gunners were then in the First Division, while their opponents were in the Third Division.

2   **Walsall 2–0 Arsenal, FA Cup third round, 1933** Another Third Division outfit felled the mighty Gunners here.

3   **Arsenal 1–2 Norwich City, FA Cup fourth round, 1953** This time the Third Division visitors knocked out First Division title-holders Arsenal.

4   **Arsenal 2–2 Bedford Town, FA Cup third round, 1956** Non-League Bedford (then of the Southern League) held the First Division Gunners.

5   **Northampton Town 3–1 Arsenal, FA Cup third round, 1958** Another Third Division side left the Gunners with red faces.

6   **Swindon Town 3–1 Arsenal, League Cup Final, 1969** The Gunners seemed set for the Cup but were beaten by Third Division Swindon.

7   **Arsenal 1–2 Walsall, League Cup fourth round, 1983** Manager Terry Neill parted company with the Club in the wake of this shock.

8   **York City 1–0 Arsenal, FA Cup third round, 1985** A Keith Houchen penalty sent the Gunners out of the Cup here.

9   **Wrexham 2–1 Arsenal, FA Cup third round, 1992** Reigning First Division champions knocked out by the team at the bottom of the Football League. Gulp!

10   **Burnley 2–0 Arsenal, League Cup quarter-final, 2008** Two Kevin McDonald goals ended Arsenal's hopes of a semi-final place.

10 REFEREES AT FA CUP FINAL VICTORIES

	Referee	Match and score	Date
1	Tom Crew	Arsenal 2–0 Huddersfield Town	1930
2	Harry Natrass	Arsenal 1–0 Sheffield United	1936
3	H. Pearce	Arsenal 2–0 Liverpool	1950
4	Norman Burtenshaw	Arsenal 2–1 Liverpool	1971
5	Ron Challis	Arsenal 3–2 Manchester United	1979
6	Keren Barratt	Arsenal 2–1 Sheffield United	1993
7	Paul Durkin	Arsenal 2–0 Newcastle United	1998
8	Mike Riley	Arsenal 2–0 Chelsea	2002
9	Graham Barber	Arsenal 1–0 Southampton	2003
10	Rob Styles	Arsenal 0–0 Manchester United (Arsenal won 5–4 on penalties)	2005

10 GREAT FA YOUTH CUP
CAMPAIGNS

	Season	Position
1	1957–58	Semi-finalists
2	1958–59	Semi-finalists
3	1960–61	Semi-finalists
4	1964–65	Runners-up
5	1965–66	Winners
6	1970–71	Winners
7	1987–88	Winners
8	1993–94	Winners
9	1999–2000	Winners
10	2000–01	Winners

The team that made the 1983–84 semi-final was skippered by future
Gunners first-team captain Tony Adams. It also included future League
Championship winners Martin Keown, Michael Thomas and David
Rocastle. Also in the team were Martin Hayes and Niall Quinn.

	Match and score	Date
1	Arsenal 7–0 Leeds United	4/9/1979
2	Arsenal 6–0 Sheffield United	23/9/2008
3=	Arsenal 5–0 Gillingham	28/9/1966
=	Arsenal 5–0 Rotherham United	3/10/1973
=	Arsenal 5–0 Chester City	9/10/1991
=	Arsenal 5–0 Hartlepool	3/10/1996
7=	Arsenal 5–1 Blackpool	29/10/1968
=	Arsenal 5–1 Wolverhampton Wanderers	2/12/2003
9=	Arsenal 4–0 Ipswich Town	28/9/1970
=	Arsenal 4–0 Newcastle	6/10/1971

Match and score	Date
1= Scunthorpe United 1–6 Arsenal	25/9/1968
= Plymouth Argyle 1–6 Arsenal	3/10/1990
3= Huddersfield Town 0–5 Arsenal	21/9/1993
= Hartlepool 0–5 Arsenal	21/9/1994
5 Liverpool 3–6 Arsenal	9/1/2006
6= Sunderland 0–3 Arsenal	25/10/2005
= Norwich City 0–3 Arsenal	10/11/1993
= Hartlepool 0–3 Arsenal	19/9/1996
= Sheffield United 0–3 Arsenal	31/10/2007
10 Rotherham United 1–3 Arsenal	29/8/1978

10 GUNNERS WHO WON EUROPEAN CUPS WITH OTHER CLUBS

	Player	Club	Match
1	**Viv Anderson**	Nottingham Forest	v Malmo, 1979; v Hamburg, 1980
2	**Nicolas Anelka**	Real Madrid	v Valencia, 2000
3	**Andy Cole**	Manchester United	v Bayern Munich, 1999
4	**Nwankwo Kanu**	Ajax	v AC Milan, 1995
5	**Ray Kennedy**	Liverpool	v Borussia Mönchengladbach, 1977
6	**Brian Kidd**	Manchester United	v Benfica, 1968
7	**Marc Overmars**	Ajax	v AC Milan, 1995
8	**Jimmy Rimmer**	Aston Villa	v Bayern Munich, 1982
9	**Davor Suker**	Real Madrid	v Juventus, 1998
10	**Tony Woodcock**	Nottingham Forest	v Malmo, 1979

10 HIGH-SCORING EUROPEAN WINS AT HOME

	Match and score	Date
1	Arsenal 7–0 Slavia Prague	23/10/2007
2	Arsenal 6–1 Austria Vienna	18/9/1991
3	Arsenal 5–1 Rosenborg	7/12/2004
4	Arsenal 4–0 FC Twente	27/8/2008
5=	Arsenal 3–0 Sparta Prague	2/11/2005
=	Arsenal 3–0 Sparta Prague	29/8/2007
7	Arsenal 4–2 Sparta Prague	25/10/2000
8=	Arsenal 3–1 AIK Solna	22/9/1999
=	Arsenal 3–1 Juventus	4/12/2001
=	Arsenal 3–1 Hamburg	21/11/2006

THE 10 HIGHEST GOAL
TALLIES IN TESTIMONIALS

	Match and score	Date	Player
1	Arsenal 8–5 International XI	8/5/1996	Paul Merson
2	Arsenal 4–4 Manchester United	17/5/1993	David O'Leary
3	Arsenal 2–5 Tottenham Hotspur	13/10/1990	Graham Rix
4	Arsenal 6–0 England XI	22/7/2006	Martin Keown
5	Arsenal 3–3 Rangers	13/5/1997	Nigel Winterburn
6	Arsenal 5–0 Hadjuk Split	10/5/1977	John Radford
7	Arsenal 2–3 Tottenham Hotspur	8/5/1985	Pat Jennings
8	Arsenal 3–1 Real Madrid	8/11/1999	Lee Dixon
9	Arsenal 2–2 Rest of London	6/5/1916	Bob Benson
10	Arsenal 2–2 Rangers	20/5/1963	Jack Kelsey

	Draws	First Season	Total seasons
1	18	1969–70	1
2	17	1993–94	1
3	16	1936–37	3
4	15	1927–28	4
5	14	1920–21	3
6	13	1928–29	5
7	12	1907–08	1
8	11	1929–30	13
9	10	1908–09	14
10	9	1904–05	17

THE 10 HIGHEST LEAGUE FINISHES IN WARTIME SEASONS*

	Season	League	Position
1	1939–40	League South 'A' Division	1st
2	1941–42	London League	1st
3	1942–43	Football League – South	1st
4	1918–19	London Combination	2nd
5	1915–16	London Combination	3rd
6	1940–41	South Regional League	4th
7	1943–44	Football League – South	4th
8	1916–17	London Combination	5th
9	1944–45	Football League – South	8th
10	1945–46	Football League South	11th

* Source: *The Official Illustrated History of Arsenal.*

THE 10 AVERAGE LEAGUE FINISHES IN THE 20TH-CENTURY

	Decade	Average League finish
1	1930s	3.5
2	1990s	4.6
3	1980s	5.3
4	1950s	6.1
5	1940s	6.3
6	1970s	8.3
7	1960s	9.6
8	1910s	11
9	1920s	11.8
10	1900s	17.3

THE 10 HIGHEST-SCORING CHAMPIONSHIP-WINNING SEASONS

	Season	Goals
1	1930–31	127
2	1932–33	118
3	1934–35	115
4	1952–53	97
5	1947–48	81
6	2001–02	79
7	1937–38	77
8	1933–34	75
9	1990–91	74
10	1988–89	73

THE 10 HIGHEST-SCORING SEASONS*

	Season	Goals
1	1930–31	127
2	1932–33	118
3	1934–35	115
4	1952–53	97
5=	1931–32	90
=	1963–64	90
7	1958–59	88
8	1925–26	87
9	1962–63	86
10	1927–28	82

* Source: *The Arsenal Factfile.*

THE 10 LOWEST-SCORING SEASONS*

	Season	Goals
1	1912–13	26
2	1904–05	36
3	1909–10	37
4	1900–01	39
5	1923–24	40
6	1910–11	41
7	1924–25	46
8=	1921–22	47
=	1974–75	47
=	1975–76	47

* Source: *The Arsenal Factfile*.

THE 10 HIGHEST-CONCEDING SEASONS*

	Season	Goals
1=	1957–58	82
=	1963–64	82
3	1959–60	80
4	1962–63	77
5=	1964–65	75
=	1965–66	75
7	1912–13	74
8	1953–54	73
9=	1928–29	72
=	1961–62	72

* Source: *The Arsenal Factfile*.

THE 10 LOWEST-CONCEDING SEASONS*

	Season	Goals
1	1903–04	22
2	1901–02	26
3	1968–69	27
4	1993–94	28
5	1970–71	29
6=	1947–48	32
=	1995–96	32
=	1996–97	32
9	1997–98	33
10=	1900–01	35
=	1986–87	35

* Source: *The Arsenal Factfile*.

THE 10 BESTSELLING ITEMS AT OFFICIAL CLUB SHOPS*

1   Adult home shirt (years 2008–10)
2   Adult away shirt (years 2008–09)
3   Youth home shirt (years 2008–10)
4   Junior home shirt (years 2008–10)
5   Adult home shirt (years 2006–08)
6   Ladies' home shirt (years 2008–10)
7   Adult long-sleeve home shirt (years 2008–10)
8   Third shirt adult (years 2008–09)
9   Toddler home kit (years 2008–10)
10   Bar scarf

* 2008 figures.

1 Andrey **ARSHAVIN**

1 Cesc **FABREGAS**

2 Theo **WALCOTT**

3 Samir **NASRI**

4 Robin **VAN PERSIE**

5 Emmanuel **ADEBAYOR**

6 **EDUARDO**

7 Gael **CLICHY**

8 Carlos **VELA**

9 Tomas **ROSICKY**

* These are predicted figures from the Arsenal licensing department as of May 2009.

TOP 10 GOALSCORERS
FROM THE 1970–71
DOUBLE CAMPAIGN*

	Player	Goals
1	Ray Kennedy	21
2	John Radford	17
3	George Graham	12
4	Charlie George	10
5	Geordie Armstrong	7
6	Peter Storey	6
7=	Eddie Kelly	5
=	Frank McLintock	5
9	own goals	2
10=	Jon Sammels	1
=	Peter Simpson	1

* These figures relate to League and FA Cup matches only – those which contributed to the 'Double'.

TOP 10 GOALSCORERS
FROM THE 1997–98
DOUBLE CAMPAIGN*

	Player	Goals
1	Dennis Bergkamp	19
2	Marc Overmars	14
3	Ian Wright	10
4	Nicolas Anelka	9
5	Ray Parlour	6
6	Christopher Wreh	4
7=	Tony Adams	3
=	David Platt	3
9=	Stephen Hughes	2
=	Emmanuel Petit	2
=	Patrick Vieira	2
=	own goals	2

* These figures relate to League and FA Cup matches only – those which contributed to the 'Double'.

TOP 10 GOALSCORERS FROM THE 2001–02 DOUBLE CAMPAIGN*

	Player	Goals
1	Thierry Henry	25
2	Freddie Ljungberg	14
3=	Dennis Bergkamp	12
=	Sylvain Wiltord	12
5	Robert Pires	10
6	Nwankwo Kanu	5
7	Sol Campbell	3
8=	Ashley Cole	2
=	Edu	2
=	Francis Jeffers	2
=	Lauren	2
=	Patrick Vieira	2

* These figures relate to League and FA Cup matches only – those which contributed to the 'Double'.

Freddie Ljungberg's second place in this Top 10 is impressive given that he is a midfielder. Many of his strikes were vital ones too, coming in the run-in. In April alone he opened the scoring in the Premiership victories against Tottenham, Ipswich, West Ham and Bolton Wanderers. He also netted in the FA Cup Final against Chelsea.

	Player	Goals
1	Thierry Henry	39
2	Robert Pires	23
3	Freddie Ljungberg	10
4	Jose Antonio Reyes	8
5	Dennis Bergkamp	7
6	Gilberto	4
7=	Jermaine Pennant	3
=	Patrick Vieira	3
=	Sylvain Wiltord	3
10	Edu	2

10 MONTHLY GOAL AVERAGES PER GAME FOR THE 2003–04 SEASON*

	Month	Average
1	August	1.33
2	September	1.33
3	October	1.66
4	November	2.25
5	December	1.40
6	January	2.33
7	February	2.20
8	March	1.66
9	April	2.75
10	May	1.00

	Player	Time	Games
1	Thierry Henry	4,312 minutes	48
2	Jens Lehmann	4,230 minutes	47
3	Kolo Toure	4,174 minutes	47 + 1
4	Ashley Cole	3,652 minutes	41
5	Lauren	3,553 minutes	39 + 2
6	Robert Pires	3,432 minutes	40 + 5
7	Sol Campbell	3,420 minutes	38
8	Gilberto	3,131 minutes	36 + 3
9	Patrick Vieira	2,966 minutes	34
9	Freddie Ljungberg	2,851 minutes	35 + 4

* Source: *The All-New Arsenal Miscellany*.

	Match and score	Date
1	Sparta Prague 0–2 Arsenal	18/10/2005
2	Arsenal 3–0 Sparta Prague	2/11/2005
3	FC Thun 0–1 Arsenal	22/11/2005
4	Arsenal 0–0 Ajax	7/12/2005
5	Real Madrid 0–1 Arsenal	21/2/2006
6	Arsenal 0–0 Real Madrid	8/3/2006
7	Arsenal 2–0 Juventus	28/3/2006
8	Juventus 0–0 Arsenal	5/4/2006
9	Arsenal 1–0 Villarreal	19/4/2006
10	Villarreal 0–0 Arsenal	25/4/2006

10 LATE GOALS

1. **Ray Kennedy v Tottenham Hotspur, May 1971 (League)**
   Kennedy's winner two minutes from time sealed the League
   Championship for Arsenal at the home of their local rivals. Sweet.

2. **Alan Sunderland v Manchester United, May 1979 (FA Cup)**
   The Gunners had been sailing to victory with a 2–0 lead, but United
   levelled the scoreline with two late strikes. Sunderland netted the
   winner to cap a balmy conclusion to the Final.

3. **Paul Vaessen v Juventus, April 1980
   (European Cup Winners' Cup)**
   'Go on, Paul, knock one in for us,' said Don Howe as he sent on 18-
   year-old Vaessen. With the score at 0–0 the Gunners were due to
   exit the competition on away goals. Vaessen duly headed past Dino
   Zoff and the Gunners marched to the Final.

4. **Michael Thomas v Liverpool, May 1989 (League)**
   The goal that sealed the League title with virtually the last kick of the
   League season.

5. **Andy Linighan v Sheffield Wednesday, May 1993 (FA Cup)**
   The replay of the Final looked set to be going to a penalty shoot-out
   when Linighan headed home a Merson corner to win the Cup for
   Arsenal.

6. **Stefan Schwarz v Sampdoria, April 1995
   (European Cup Winners' Cup)**
   Minutes from a heartbreaking defeat at the hands of the Italians, the
   Swede scored from a free-kick to hand aggregate advantage to
   Arsenal. One spectacular penalty shoot-out later and the Gunners
   were in their second successive Final in the competition.

7 David Platt v Manchester United, 1997 (Premiership)
'Great header, David Platt,' said the commentator as the midfielder nodded home a Nigel Winterburn corner. This capped an Arsenal comeback after they had thrown away a two-goal lead. It also swung the title race back in their favour.

8 Martin Keown v Shakhtar Donetsk, September 2000 (UEFA Champions League)
The visitors went 2–0 up in the first half and seemed certain to win. A Wiltord penalty handed Arsenal a lifeline, then Keown of all people scored twice in the final six minutes to win the tie.

9 Thierry Henry v Manchester United, November 2001 (Premiership)
With the scoreline seemingly locked at 1–1, the final ten minutes of this match proved fruitful for Henry. He capitalized on two errors from fellow-countryman Fabien Barthez – a mis-hit clearance and a dropped ball – to give the Gunners a 3–1 victory.

10 Ashley Cole v Dynamo Kiev, November 2003 (UEFA Champions League)
After a frustrating night of football, Arsenal were 90 seconds away from being knocked out of the competition when Cole turned home Thierry Henry's header.

	Player	Period at Arsenal
1	David Bentley	2001–06
2	Laurie Brown	1961–64
3	Sol Campbell	2001–06
4	David Jenkins	1963–68
5	Pat Jennings	1977–85
6	Rohan Ricketts	2001–02
7	Jimmy Robertson	1968–76
8	Kevin Stead	1978
9	Steve Walford	1977–80
10	Willie Young	1976–81

10 EARLY ST TOTTERINGHAM'S DAYS*

	Date	Season
1	9 March	2007–08
2	13 March	2003–04
3	18 March	2001–02
4	24 March	2002–03
5	26 March	1993–94
6	28 March	1997–98
7	2 April	2004–05
8	3 April	1997–98
9	3 April	1990–91
10	7 April	1972–73

* When Arsenal fans celebrate the fact that Tottenham Hotspur can't catch them up that season.

10 HIGH HOME WINS AGAINST TOTTENHAM HOTSPUR

	Match and score	Date
1	Arsenal 5–1 Tottenham Hotspur	20/10/1934
2	Arsenal 4–0 Tottenham Hotspur	7/2/1953
3	Arsenal 4–0 Tottenham Hotspur	16/9/1967
4	Arsenal 3–0 Tottenham Hotspur	8/1/1949
5	Arsenal 3–0 Tottenham Hotspur	16/11/2002
6	Arsenal 3–0 Tottenham Hotspur	2/12/2006
7	Arsenal 3–1 Tottenham Hotspur	26/12/1911
8	Arsenal 3–1 Tottenham Hotspur	20/10/1956
9	Arsenal 3–1 Tottenham Hotspur	13/9/1958
10	Arsenal 3–1 Tottenham Hotspur	23/2/1965

	Match and score	Date
1	Arsenal 8–1 Liverpool	1/9/1934
2	Arsenal 6–0 Liverpool	28/11/1931
3	Arsenal 5–0 Liverpool	2/2/1909
4	Arsenal 4–0 Liverpool	20/4/1992
5	Arsenal 6–3 Liverpool	7/3/1928
6	Arsenal 3–0 Liverpool	10/4/1954
7	Arsenal 3–0 Liverpool	2/12/1990
8	Arsenal 3–0 Liverpool	12/11/2006
9	Arsenal 5–3 Liverpool	4/4/1953
10	Arsenal 3–1 Liverpool	1/3/1924

	Match and score	**Date**
1	Arsenal 5–0 Manchester United	30/1/1937
2	Arsenal 6–2 Manchester United	1/2/1947
3	Arsenal 5–1 Manchester United	8/1/1898*
4	Arsenal 5–1 Manchester United	3/12/1898*
5	Arsenal 4–0 Manchester United	3/10/1903
6	Arsenal 4–0 Manchester United	16/3/1907
7	Arsenal 4–0 Manchester United	22/8/1970
8	Arsenal 4–0 Manchester United	5/11/2001
9	Arsenal 5–2 Manchester United	23/4/1960
10	Arsenal 4–1 Manchester United	21/2/1931

* Manchester United were known as Newton Heath at this time.

TOM WATT'S 10
NORTH BANK HEROES*

1   **Charles Buchan** The Laundry End's first proper superstar.

2   **Alex James** Coming down Saturday for 'a bob's worth of Alex'?

3   **Danny Clapton** One bright light in the late 1950s gloom.

4   **Charlie George** Born is the king of Highbury.

5   **Willie Young** The biggest Willie in the land.

6   **Liam Brady** We all agree, Brady was better than Hoddle.

7   **Charlie Nicholas** Who always saved his very best for Tottenham.

8   **Tony Adams** Mr Arsenal.

9   **David Rocastle** Oh, Rocky, Rocky – we'll never forget him, one of our own.

10 **Ian Wright** So good they named him three times – 'Ian Wright, Wright, Wright!'

* Tom Watt is a writer and actor.

PAUL KAYE'S 10 MOMENTS GUARANTEED TO MAKE YOU SMILE*

1   Martin Keown at Old Trafford
There is just something utterly wonderful about watching a footballer playing in a huge game in front of a global TV audience of billions behave like a seven-year-old boy in a school playground.

2   Henry and Pires's 'trick penalty' v Manchester City
Two of the most gifted footballers ever to grace this country conspire to create the most embarrassing penalty of all time. Truly, truly painful to watch, but hilarious nonetheless.

3   Ian Wright 'just do it . . . again!'
When Ian Wright took off his shirt to reveal a vest saying 279 goals scored . . . only for him to realize that he had in fact only scored 278, his reaction truly personified the man. He just got the ball and went up and scored another one. No biggie.

4   The squirrel
The Arsenal players are on the rampage towards the Villereal box up at the Clock End during the home leg of the Champions League semi-final and almost every single spectator crammed into Highbury that night was looking the other way. Why? Well, er . . . there was a squirrel sniffing a corner flag down at the North Bank. The power of the squirrel should not be underestimated.

5   Pizzagate
Right up there with all the best 'gates' (Watergate, Manuelgate and Heavens Gate), the young Spanish wizard Cesc Fabregas, conducts an interesting experiment to test the reaction of the tabloid press when you throw a concoction of dough, melted cheese and anchovies at a cranky old hairdryer.

6   **Steve Morrow**

It's hard to spoil a moment as special as winning your first trophy at Wembley, but getting lifted up by your captain at the final whistle for scoring the winning goal and then flipping backwards over his shoulder, breaking your arm in two places, will do it every time.

7   **Fabien Barthez**

The first gaff from Fabien that wonderful day against United was a sheer delight, but the second sent us howling into ecstasy. The icing on the cake, however, was seeing his face morphed on to the body of a Clanger in the *Sun* the following day.

8   **Tony flicking the Vs at Loftus Road**

Not having been at Loftus Road that day, I was outraged at suggestions in the media that our glorious leader had 'flicked the Vs' at the Queens Park Rangers fans. In fact, he had – lots of them. He turned 360 degrees, flicking them wildly at all four stands of the ground for good measure.

9   **Lee Dixon's own goal v Coventry**

If you're going to score an own goal you might as well make it a belter. In the good old days back in 1998, you could actually enjoy an own goal like this, safe in the knowledge that we'd be banging in four or five up the other end.

10   **Sammy Nelson's arse-nal**

I was on the North Bank the day Sammy Nelson dropped his shorts at us, but thankfully I was too short to see what was going on and was left untraumatized by the incident.

* Paul Kaye is an actor, comedian and writer.

1   Theo Walcott
Young, fit and strong, he has vision and has shown great potential, which he's now beginning to deliver on. Looks great in Armani.

2   Thierry Henry
An artist, he can seem out of a game for 89 minutes and then turn on a sixpence and volley the United keeper from 23 yards. Would probably make a nice breakfast.

3   Tony Adams
A rock, passionate and a born leader. Poetic through life experiences. If Arsenal were a man, then that man would be Adams.

4   Freddie Ljungberg
Committed, tenacious attacking midfielder, somewhat mercurial. A great servant to the Club through an epoch-making passage in our history. Looks absolutely fabulous in his underwear.

5   Cesc Fabregas
Creative genius, mature, deeply talented yet massively understated. A linchpin, a midfield general, a phenomenon. Occasional issues with dodgy sideburns, but his boyish good looks make him handsome enough for any top ten.

6   Martin Keown
In a word, rugged. The strong, silent type. Committed, a man to be relied on. A team player who, when cut, would bleed Arsenal.

7 Charlie Nicholas

Full of Glaswegian charm, his hairstyle alone revolutionized the old First Division. A mop hair player whose flair on the field didn't stop off it. You'll never be short of a glass of the fizzy stuff with Champagne Charlie around.

8 Charlie George

Not a looker, but remember that celebration in the 1971 FA Cup Final? And that long, lustrous hair . . .

9 David Seaman

Alongside big Bob Wilson, the finest keeper at our club – a man who won us titles. And while the ponytail had its dissenters, we all know that it's fun to stay in the YMCA.

10 George Graham

Well groomed, fantastic suits.

* '...if I was that way inclined.' Hardeep Singh Kohli is a comedian, writer and broadcaster.

M PEOPLE STAR SHOVELL'S TOP 10 FAN CHANTS

1 **'Good old Arsenal'** This is the song the Arsenal should run out to. This song is historic, famous and proud – just like the Club.

2 **'She wore a yellow ribbon'** The Arsenal on a good FA Cup run, with this song being sung by thousands of us, hairs on the back of the neck time.

3 **'Jesus said Paddy'** A favourite away-day Cup song for all those in the know – proper history. Woooah!

4 **'Charlie Charlie, born is the king of Highbury'** Charlie George, 'nuf said.

5 **'We all agree, Rixy is better than Hoddle'** We called it as we saw it.

6 **'1–0 to the Arsenal'** 1994 in Denmark, European silverware in the bag and roaring this one out. A perfect end to a perfect evening. Still a favourite.

7 **'Walking in a Bergkamp wonderland'** A Dutch artist who had the sublime touch of a genius on the football pitch. Absolute class, a proper legend of the Arsenal.

8 **'Vieira wooh o aoh Vieira'** Along with songs for the likes of Tony Adams, Thierry Henry and Ian Wright, this is a favourite. These are proper Arsenal boys, leaders of men who wore the shirt with pride. Legends.

9 **'The Arsenal: clap clap clap! The Arsenal: clap clap clap!'** This is who we are. Sing it loud and sing it clear!

10 **'Yellow, yellow, yellow'** In honour of all the Arsenal away boys.

ROBERT PESTON'S TOP 10 ARSENAL MEMORIES FROM THE 1970S*

1. Bob Wilson, Pat Rice, Bob McNab, Frank McLintock, Peter Simpson, Peter Storey, George Graham, George Armstrong, Charlie George, Ray Kennedy, John Radford.

2. Charlie George on his back after the screamer that clinched the Double.

3. The advent of Liam Brady and the rebirth of hope.

4. Pride in Herbert Chapman and our great history.

5. Peter Storey's stoppage-time penalty equalizer against Stoke City in the 1971 FA Cup semi-final, without which there would not have been a Double.

6. The ineffable superiority of having been born into an Arsenal household rather than a Spurs one.

7. The schoolboy enclosure, where my sister and I could stand without Dad.

8. Itchy, knitted red-and-white bobblehats.

9. The screaming yellow of that away kit.

10. The all-pervading smell of fried onions, lukewarm beefburgers and cheap cigars during the mobbed walk from Finsbury Park to Highbury.

* Robert Peston, the BBC's Economics Correspondent, grew up in north London and started supporting Arsenal as a child.

1. **John Hollins** He signed from QPR the day before his 33rd birthday, played for another four years and was voted Player of the Year in 1981–82.

2. **Jock Rutherford** The winger holds the record as the Club's oldest player thanks to his appearance against Manchester City in March 1926 at the age of 41 years 159 days.

3. **John Lukic** He had two separate spells with the Gunners and kept goal against Lazio in 2000, just short of his 40th birthday.

4. **Nigel Winterburn** Having been written off by some, the left back went on to win the Double under Arsène Wenger in 1998.

5. **Martin Keown** In 2004 the tough centre back won a Premiership winners' medal at the age of 37.

6. **Leslie Compton** The football and cricket legend retired a few months before his 40th birthday.

7. **Dennis Bergkamp** Age did not wither the Dutchman. He was class personified right into his final game at 37.

8. **David O'Leary** In his 36th year the Irishman bowed out gracefully with a freshly won FA Cup winners' medal in his hand.

9. **Paul Davis** The midfielder lost none of his class into his 30s, as he showed during the 1993–94 European Cup Winners' Cup campaign.

10. **Ian Wright** He was as energetic as ever when he won a Premiership medal at 34 and retired just short of his 37th birthday.

* Chris is BBC *Breakfast News* Sports Reporter and son of Arsenal's John Hollins.

STEVE BOULD'S
10 DEFENSIVE GIANTS*

1   Tony Adams
2   Sol Campbell
3   Lee Dixon
4   Martin Keown
5   Frank McLintock
6   David O'Leary
7   Emmanuel Petit
8   Pat Rice
9   Kenny Sansom
10 Nigel Winterburn

* Having played a total of 371 games for the Gunners, centre back Steve Bould won three League Championships with the Club. He is now head coach of Arsenal's U18 Academy side.

1 **15/8/1970** Opening day point: a difficult game at Goodison against the champions Everton in which Charlie George broke two bones in his ankle. George Graham snatched the late, late equalizer in a 2–2 draw.

2 **22/8/1970** Manchester United humbled: at Highbury the first home game of the season beating of Best, Charlton, Law and Co. convinced us that the 1970 European Fairs Cup triumph was no fluke.

3 **26/9/1970** Wake-up call in the Potteries: how and why this 5–0 defeat happened is a mystery, although Stoke had a brilliant day. Our response was crucial – 14 League games unbeaten and the chase of leaders Leeds United was back on.

4 **26/12/1970** After a pretty boring 0–0 home draw against Southampton we were all in the bath when our brilliant winger George Armstrong assessed our chances. 'We're going to win the lot because we are not only a great team now but have luck on our side as well. You win nothing without luck. Bet we win the Double.'

5 **6/1/1971** The FA Cup glory starts at non-League Yeovil Town. Skipper Frank McLintock and I are wound up by the Yeovil chairman's remarks about us: 'McLintock's too old and goalie Wilson is slow to fast balls.' Another good reply as we kept a clean sheet against the Southern League team, winning 3–0 on the awkward sloping ground against tricky opponents.

6 **17/2/1971** Charlie's back! A fifth-round FA Cup tie at Maine Road, home of Manchester City, on a mud heap of a pitch, saw Charlie George win the game with two goals on his return from

injury. Frank McLintock goaded Charlie, telling him City's flamboyant coach, Malcolm Allison, had dismissed him as an 'upstart'.

7　**27/3/1971** Coach and skipper's half time rant at Hillsborough. All hopes of an improbable Double seemed shot in this FA Cup semi-final against Stoke. At 2–0 down, it took the inspirational belief of Don Howe and Frank's 'never say die' approach to turn the game on its head. A 2–2 draw and a comfortable 2–0 replay win took us to Wembley and the Final.

8　**3/5/1971** Champions at White Hart Lane – a Roy of the Rovers script could never replicate this amazing event. Any win and a 0–0 draw against our old enemy would bring us the title; 1–1 or 2–2 etc. and it would go to Leeds. Ray Kennedy's late header fulfilled all our dreams in the 1–0 win. We were champions of England.

9　**8/5/1971** FA Cup Final day and the Double. The memory is of an iconic winner from an iconic Arsenal man: local boy Charlie George completes the fairytale for us, 111 minutes into the game.

10　**9/5/1971** The homecoming: unbelievable scenes of joy as half a million people lined the streets of Islington from Highbury to the town hall. Two trophies on show, the coveted Double won and the normally reserved Bertie Mee waving and smiling, while our charismatic, extrovert leader, Frank McLintock, sits totally exhausted and almost asleep on the town hall steps.

* A key member of the Double-winning side of 1971, Wilson kept goal for Arsenal in 308 games. He is the co-founder of the Willow Foundation charity (website: www.willowfoundation.org.uk).

1   **Arsenal 4–2 Southampton, 23/9/1995**
I scored my first two Arsenal goals in this match and so it's obviously a memorable game for me. I was so pleased to get my first goal.

2   **Arsenal 3–1 Tottenham Hotspur, 24/11/1996**
This was not my first game against Tottenham but it was the one where I really grasped what the rivalry means to the fans. I scored a goal late in the game and during the celebration that followed I realized what Arsenal means and what English football means.

3   **Leicester City 3–3 Arsenal, 27/8/1997**
I didn't score many hat-tricks in my career. This was the most memorable. All three of the goals were fairly good.

4   **Arsenal 5–0 Leicester City, 20/2/1999**
Anelka scored a hat-trick in this game and I set up several goals. It just clicked on the day. Afterwards, Arsène Wenger said he had never seen anyone play so well without scoring. That meant a lot to me.

5   **Tottenham Hotspur 2–2 Arsenal, 25/4/2004**
I respect all opponents, but I knew what it would mean to the fans to win the Premiership at White Hart Lane. We put together some great moves and on the day a point was enough to make us champions. I feel the way we celebrated was very respectful and the whole experience was neat.

6   **Arsenal 5–3 Middlesbrough, 22/8/2004**
Early in the second half of this tie we were 3–1 down and I took this personally because I was captain that day. I scored the goal that brought us back to 3–2 and from there we did the most amazing comeback to win 5–3. It felt great to have led such a comeback.

7   Arsenal 7–0 Everton, 11/5/2005
We seemed to put in so many great performances against Everton at Highbury. In this one I was on great form. I set up several goals and scored one myself.

8   Arsenal 3–1 West Bromwich Albion, 15/4/2006
The Club was giving each home game a theme that season and this one was Dennis Bergkamp Day. The fans were amazingly nice that day and turned the stadium orange. I was a little embarrassed as I sometimes feel uncomfortable with the limelight, but when I came on as a substitute and scored that felt very special.

9   Arsenal 4–2 Wigan Athletic, 7/5/2006
This was my final competitive game for Arsenal and the Club's final game at Highbury. For me, although I had a sniff of the Emirates in my testimonial, Arsenal means Highbury because it was there where I played for the Club. Actually, my final game for Ajax was also the final game for them in their old stadium.

10   Arsenal 2–1 Ajax, 22/7/2006
This was my testimonial and was special for so many reasons. It was the first game at the Emirates Stadium, my father kicked off the game, and my wife and children were involved with the day too. So many legends came back to take part. A wonderful day.

* Between 1995 and 2006, Dutchman Bergkamp played 423 games for Arsenal. During that time the Club won numerous trophies, including Doubles in 1998 and 2002.

KENNY SANSOM'S TOP 10 PLAYERS*

1 **Steve Bould** He's so underrated. I'd put him on a par with Tony Adams. When you speak to football fans, they rate him so much.

2 **Gus Caesar** He had no first touch. His first touch was a volley! But he had a good character and worked hard. He was great fun.

3 **John Devine** What a great player and a fantastic character.

4 **Pat Jennings** Simply the best goalkeeper around. We called him 'God'. He made saves no other keeper could.

5 **Niall Quinn** I've so much respect for Niall. I played with him in the reserves and that is where you find out about people. A great footballer.

6 **Graham Rix** He was a fantastic player who had an incredible understanding of those around him.

7 **David Rocastle** I remember playing against him when I was at Newcastle United. He knew me so well. He told me, 'Kenny, I can never beat you.' It was true, he couldn't. But what a legend.

8 **Frank Stapleton** A fantastic centre forward. He was a team player and held the ball up well for his team-mates. Team players are so important and he was a great one.

9 **Brian Talbot** He would do everything to be the best. He would work, work, work. And he got his rewards.

10 **Paul Vaessen** He was a really good kid. He lost his way, it is true, but he deserves to be remembered as a good player and for that goal against Juventus.

* Former Club captain Sansom played 394 games for Arsenal. He won the League Cup medal in 1987.

ARSENAL LEGENDS' LISTS

10 HIGH POINTS TALLIES*

	Season	Points
1	2003–04	90
2	2001–02	87
3	2004–05	83
4	1997–98	78
5	1998–99	78
6	2002–03	78
7	1988–89	76
8	1999–2000	73
9	1991–92	72
10	1981–82	71

* All the seasons in this list came after the introduction of three points for a win in 1981–82 (prior to this just two points were awarded for a win). Had the three points applied throughout the Club's history the top campaign would have been the 1970–71 season in which the Club would have amassed 94 points.

10 LOW POINTS TALLIES

	Season	Points
1	1912–13	18
2	1893–94	28
3	1909–10	31
4	1895–96	32
5	1904–05	33
6	1923–24	33
7	1924–25	33
8	1894–95	34
9	1899–1900	36
10	1907–08	36

* All the seasons in this list came prior to the introduction of three points for a win in 1981–82, when only two points were awarded for a win.

10 HIGH-SELLING
HIGHBURY AUCTION LOTS*

	Lot	Price
1	George Graham's old desk and chair	£25,000
2	Match sign from final match against Wigan	£11,000
3	Last programme off the production line for final match against Wigan	£7,500
4	Sign signalling first Highbury match on 6/9/1913 v Leicester Fosse	£5,000
5	Tray with classic Art Deco AFC symbol	£4,750
6	Photo of Arsène Wenger from 1998 Double year	£4,000
7	Alloy Arsenal cannon sign	£2,800
8	Arsène Wenger's dugout seat	£1,600
9	Wax dummy of George Graham	£800
10	Centre circle	£500

* When Arsenal left Highbury in 2006, auctions were held of stadium memorabilia.

1   **Abou Diaby** secured the first of the 60,000 seats on 13/3/2006.

2   **Sir Robert McAlpine Ltd** was appointed to carry out construction work.

3   Designed by **HOK Sport,** who are also architects of Stadium Australia in Sydney, the English National Stadium Wembley, Royal Ascot Racecourse and Wimbledon Centre Court.

4   Arsenal's award-winning groundsman **Paul Burgess** was fully involved in pitch matters.

5   **Patrick Vieira** and **Thierry Henry** placed the time capsule in the stadium.

6   **Young Arsenal fans** designed 'Play Safe' posters to display on hoardings.

7   Manager **Arsène Wenger** was closely involved in every aspect of the design of players' facilities.

8   Director **Danny Fizman** helped connect the two halves of the first main truss at the stadium.

9   The **Royal Bank of Scotland** headed the consortium of banks that gave the Club the initial loan package to fund construction.

10 The stadium was officially opened by **Prince Philip, Duke of Edinburgh,** on 26/10/2006.

10 FINAL-DAY HIGHLIGHTS AT HIGHBURY

1   **Thierry Henry** kissing the turf to celebrate his hat-trick.

2   **Arsène Wenger** leading the supporters in counting down the final ten seconds on the Highbury clock.

3   **Playing legends** from the Club's time at Highbury appearing on the pitch.

4   The Who frontman **Roger Daltrey** singing 'Highbury Highs'.

5   Thierry Henry being presented with the **Golden Boot**.

6   **Giant models** of Tony Adams, Dennis Bergkamp, Thierry Henry and Arsène Wenger being paraded round the ground.

7   The fine performance of the **Romford Drum and Trumpet Corps**.

8   Boxing legend **Henry Cooper** talking about his famous fight with Muhammad Ali at the stadium.

9   The – ahem – unsympathetic chants about **Tottenham Hotspur**'s players' food-poisoning trouble.

10 The amazing **firework display** that concluded the closing ceremony at the stadium.

10 NON-ARSENAL MATCHES
PLAYED AT HIGHBURY

	Match	Date
1	England v Rest of Europe	26/10/1938
2	Boxers v Jockeys	2/4/1951*
3	Metropolitan Police v Paris Police	3/5/1951
4	British Olympic XI v England 'B' Trial XI	30/4/1952
5	Wycombe Wanderers v Bishop Auckland (FA Amateur Cup Final)	13/4/1957
6	British Army v Belgian Army	27/3/1957
7	London Hilton Hotel v Regent Palace Hotel	12/4/1965
8	Portsmouth v Liverpool (FA Cup semi-final)	4/5/1992
9	Wimbledon v Chelsea (FA Cup semi-final)	13/4/1997
10	Barking Abbey v Ernest Bevin College	17/5/2000

* This was the first game at Highbury played under floodlights.

10 STADIUMS WHERE ARSENAL HAVE WON A MAJOR TROPHY

	Stadium	Trophy and date
1	Anfield	Championship: 1989
2	Ayresome Park	Championship: 1935
3	Highbury	Championship: 1931, 1938, 1953, 1998; Fairs Cup: 1970
4	Leeds Road	Championship: 1948
5	Millennium Stadium	FA Cup: 2002, 2003, 2005
6	Old Trafford	Championship: 2002
7	Parken Stadium, Copenhagen	European Cup Winners' Cup: 1994
8	Stamford Bridge	Championship: 1933, 1934
9	Wembley Stadium	FA Cup: 1930, 1936, 1950, 1971, 1979, 1993, 1998; League Cup: 1987, 1993
10	White Hart Lane	Championship: 1971, 2004

10 HIGHBURY TIME CAPSULE ITEMS

1. A **list** of every Arsenal player.
2. A David Rocastle **shirt**.
3. A **photograph** of Ian Wright celebrating his record-breaking strike against Bolton Wanderers on 13/9/1997.
4. A Highbury match **ticket**.
5. A piece of Highbury **turf**.
6. A copy of a **newspaper** on the day of the time capsule's burial.
7. A Highbury **flag**.
8. A **record** of every match played at Highbury.
9. A replica of the Clock End **clock**.
10. A virtual tour **video** of Highbury.

STADIUMS

10 KEY HIGHBURY DATES

1   **1913** Arsenal plays its first match at Arsenal Stadium, Highbury, beating Leicester Fosse 2–1.

2   **1915** Arsenal FC buys the stadium site outright.

3   **1932** The West Stand is opened by HRH the Prince of Wales.

4   **1935** A roof is built over the Laundry End (later renamed the North Bank).

5   **1935** A clock is installed at the back of the College End terrace (later renamed the Clock End).

6   **1936** The Art Deco-style East Stand is opened.

7   **1989** Executive boxes and the roof over the Clock End erected.

8   **1992** North Bank terrace is demolished to make way for the 12,500-seater, two-tiered North Stand.

9   **1993** The Clock End is reopened, making Highbury an all-seater stadium.

10   **2006** Demolition work begins.

10 HIGHBURY HIGHLIGHTS

	Highlight	Date
1	First competitive match at Highbury	6/9/1913
2	The renaming of Gillespie Road station	5/11/1932
3	Seven Gunners in the England team	13/11/1934
4	George Allison's side attracts record crowd	9/3/1935
5	First game under floodlights	19/9/1951
6	Henry Cooper and Muhammed Ali's world heavyweight title fight	21/5/1966
7	Arsenal wins the Fairs Cup in 1970	28/4/1970
8	Final game in front of the old North Bank	2/5/1992
9	Ian Wright breaks Cliff Bastin's goalscoring record	13/9/1997
10	Last game in red and white kit	11/5/2005

10 MILLENNIUM STADIUM
MATCHES

	Competition	Match and score
1	FA Cup Final 2001	Arsenal 1–2 Liverpool
2	Community Shield 2002	Arsenal 1–0 Liverpool
3	FA Cup Final 2002	Arsenal 2–0 Chelsea
4	FA Cup Final 2003	Arsenal 1–0 Southampton
5	Community Shield 2003	Arsenal 1–1 Manchester United (Manchester United won 4–3 on penalties)
6	Community Shield 2004	Arsenal 3–1 Manchester United
7	FA Cup semi-final 2005	Arsenal 3–0 Blackburn Rovers
8	FA Cup Final 2005	Arsenal 0–0 Manchester United (Arsenal won 5–4 on penalties)
9	Community Shield 2005	Arsenal 1–2 Chelsea
10	League Cup Final 2007	Arsenal 1–2 Chelsea

1 **Valencia 0–0 Arsenal, 14/5/1980**
European Cup Winners' Cup (Valencia won 5–4 on penalties)

2 **Millwall 1–1 Arsenal, 7/10/1992**
League Cup (Arsenal won 3–1 on penalties)

3 **Manchester United 1–1 Arsenal, 7/8/1993**
FA Charity Shield (Manchester United won 5–4 on penalties)

4 **Sampdoria 3–2 Arsenal, 20/4/1995**
European Cup Winners' Cup (5–5 on aggregate, Arsenal won
3–2 on penalties)

5 **Port Vale 1–1 Arsenal, 14/1/1998**
FA Cup (Arsenal won 4–3 on penalties)

6 **West Ham 1–1 Arsenal, 17/3/1998**
FA Cup (Arsenal won 4–3 on penalties)

7 **Middlesbrough 2–2 Arsenal, 30/11/1999**
League Cup (Middlesbrough won 3–1 on penalties)

8 **Leicester City 0–0 Arsenal, 19/1/2000**
FA Cup (Leicester City won 6–5 on penalties)

9 **Galatasaray 0–0 Arsenal, 17/5/2000**
UEFA Cup (Galatasaray won 4–1 on penalties)

10 **Manchester United 1–1, 10/8/2003**
Community Shield (Manchester United won 4–3 on penalties)

FIRST 10 OVERSEAS PLAYERS TO REPRESENT ARSENAL*

	Player	Country	Signed
1	Gerard Keyser	Netherlands	1930
2	Albert Gudmundsson	Iceland	1946
3	Dan Roux	South Africa	1957
4	John Kosmina	Australia	1978
5	Vladimir Petrovic	Yugoslavia	1982
6	Siggi Jonsson	Iceland	1989
7	Anders Limpar	Sweden	1990
8	Pal Lydersen	Denmark (Norwegian nationality)	1991
9	John Jensen	Denmark	1992
10	Stefan Schwarz	Sweden	1994

* This list does not cover overseas players who have British nationality.
Source: *The Foreign Revolution* by Nick Harris (published by Aurum Press).

FIRST 10 NON-EUROPEANS
TO REPRESENT ARSENAL

	Player	Country	Signed
1	Dan Roux	South Africa	1957
2	John Kosmina	Australia	1978
3	Jehad Muntasser	Libya	1997
4	Christopher Wreh	Liberia	1997
5	Fabian Caballero	Argentina	1998
6	Nwankwo Kanu	Nigeria	1998
7	Nelson Vivas	Argentina	1998
8	Silvinho	Brazil	1999
9	Lauren	Cameroon	2000
10	Junichi Inamoto	Japan	2001

10 ARSÈNE WENGER
FIRSTS

1   **Goal** Ian Wright v Blackburn Rovers (a), 12/10/1996

2   **Defeat** Manchester United 1–0 Arsenal, 16/11/1996

3   **Hat-trick** Dennis Bergkamp v Leicester City (a), 27/8/1997

4   **Purchase** Remi Garde and Patrick Vieira, 14/8/1996

5   **Sale** Eddie McGoldrick released to Manchester City, 18/10/1996

6   **Award** Manager of the Month, March 1998

7   **Red card** Steve Bould v Liverpool (a), 27/11/1996

8   **Home game** Arsenal 0–0 Coventry City, 19/10/1996

9   **Trophy** Premiership, secured on 3/5/1998

10 **European game** Paok Salonika 1–0 Arsenal, 16/9/1997

	Match and score	Date
1	Arsenal 0–1 Tottenham Hotspur	29/8/1925
2	Arsenal 2–2 Leicester City	31/8/1925
3	Manchester United 0–1 Arsenal	5/9/1925
4	Leicester City 0–1 Arsenal	7/9/1925
5	Arsenal 1–1 Liverpool	12/9/1925
6	Burnley 2–2 Arsenal	19/9/1925
7	Arsenal 3–2 West Ham United	21/9/1925
8	Arsenal 4–1 Leeds United	26/9/1925
9	Newcastle United 7–0 Arsenal	3/10/1925
10	West Ham United 0–4 Arsenal	5/10/1925

10 KIT HISTORY
MOMENTS

1   The first kit worn by the team is all-red, donated by goalkeeper Fred Beardsley in 1886, who once played for Nottingham Forest.

2   In 1895 the players briefly wore a new kit with red and light blue vertical stripes.

3   White sleeves were added to the kit by Herbert Chapman in March 1933.

4   In February 1936 the team took to the field wearing horizontal striped jerseys and black shorts to avoid a clash with the Barnsley players' red kits.

5   For the 1950 FA Cup Final the Gunners wore a gold kit.

6   During the 1960s the Club returned to an all-red shirt until the arrival of Bertie Mee, who reinstated the white sleeves.

7   During the 1982–83 season the Club's change strip was green and blue.

8   For the 2001–02 Double-winning campaign Arsenal wore a gold away shirt.

9   For the final season at Highbury the Club returned to a redcurrant shirt – the same colour as that worn in the first season at the stadium.

10 In 2007 the club released a white away strip in tribute to manager Herbert Chapman.

10 ARSENAL FIRSTS
FOR FOOTBALL

1 **First English club to host an international involving a non-British side** England 6–1 Belgium, 19/3/1923

2 **First club to have a League game covered on radio** Arsenal 1–1 Sheffield United, 22/1/1927

3 **First club to score a goal live on radio** Arsenal 1–1 Sheffield United, 22/1/1927

4 **Participants in the first FA Cup Final broadcast on the radio** Arsenal 0–1 Cardiff City, 23/4/1927

5 **First club to pay a five-figure transfer fee** £10,890 for David Jack, 13/10/1928

6 **First club to have a match broadcast live on television** Arsenal v Arsenal Reserves, 16/9/1937

7 **First club to play in the Soviet Union** Dynamo Moscow 0–5 Arsenal, 5/10/1954

8 **First club to score in an FA Cup Final staged outside England (Millennium Stadium, Cardiff)** Arsenal 1–2 Liverpool, 12/5/2001

9 **First club to win an FA Cup Final played 'indoors'** Arsenal 1–0 Southampton, 17/5/2003

10 **First team in English football to field a squad with no UK players** Arsenal 5–1 Crystal Palace, 14/2/2005

10 FIRSTS
FOR THE CLUB

1   **Woolwich Arsenal's first competitive League match**
    v Newcastle United, 2/9/1893 (drew 2–2)

2   **First Woolwich Arsenal FA Cup match** v Ashford United,
    14/10/1893 (won 12–0)

3   **Arsenal's first competitive match** v Bristol City, 4/4/1914
    (drew 1–1)

4   **First Charity Shield match** v Sheffield Wednesday, 8/10/1930
    (won 2–1)

5   **First competitive European match** v Staevnet, Inter-Cities Fairs
    Cup, 25/9/1963 (won 7–1)

6   **First League Cup match** v Gillingham, 13/9/1966 (drew 1–1)

7   **First European Cup Winners' Cup match** v Fenerbahçe,
    19/9/1979 (won 2–0)

8   **First Premiership match** v Norwich City, 15/8/1992 (lost 2–4)

9   **First UEFA Champions League match** v RC Lens, 16/9/1998
    (drew 1–1)

10 **First Community Shield match** v Liverpool, 11/8/2002 (won 1–0)

FIRST 10 VICTORIES OVER TOTTENHAM HOTSPUR

	Score	Match	Date
1	Arsenal 1–0 Tottenham Hotspur	Friendly	9/3/1889
2	Arsenal 10–1 Tottenham Hotspur	Friendly	28/9/1889
3	Arsenal 5–0 Tottenham Hotspur	Friendly	28/4/1898
4	Arsenal 2–1 Tottenham Hotspur	United League	11/3/1899
5	Arsenal 2–1 Tottenham Hotspur	Southern District Combination	24/4/1900
6	Arsenal 2–1 Tottenham Hotspur	London League	17/11/1902
7	Tottenham Hotspur 0–1 Arsenal	London League	1/9/1903
8	Arsenal 5–0 Tottenham Hotspur	Southern Professional Charity Cup	28/4/1906
9	Tottenham Hotspur 0–1 Arsenal	Friendly	1/2/1908
10	Arsenal 1–0 Tottenham Hotspur	Football League Division One	4/12/1909

10 EMIRATES STADIUM
FIRSTS

1   **First attendance** 60,023 v Aston Villa, 19/8/2006

2   **First referee** Graham Poll v Aston Villa, 19/8/2006

3   **First Arsenal goal** Gilberto v Aston Villa, 19/8/2006

4   **First disallowed goal** Kolo Toure v Aston Villa, 19/8/2006 (offside)

5   **First UEFA Champions League goal** Freddie Ljungberg v Dinamo Zagreb, 23/8/2006

6   **First international match** Brazil 3–0 Argentina, 3/9/2006

7   **First Premiership win** Arsenal 3–0 Sheffield Wednesday, 23/9/2006

8   **First goal against Tottenham Hotspur** Emmanuel Adebayor, 2/12/2006

9   **First goal against Manchester United** Robin van Persie, 21/1/2007

10 **First hat-trick** Jay Simpson v Cardiff City, 19/2/2007, FA Youth Cup

	Date	Opponents	Result
1	11/12/1886	Eastern Wanderers (a)	Won 6–0
2	8/1/1887	Erith (h)	Won 6–1
3	15/1/1887	Alexandria United (h)	Won 11–0
4	22/1/1887	Eastern Wanderers (h)	Won 1–0
5	29/1/1887	Erith (a)	Won 3–2
6	5/2/1887	Millwall Rovers (h)	Lost 4–0
7	12/2/1887	Alexandria United (a)	Won 6–0
8	25/2/1887	2nd Rifle Brigade (h)	Drew 0–0
9	12/3/1887	Millwall Rovers (h)	Won 3–0
10	26/3/1887	2nd Rifle Brigade (a)	Lost 1–0

FIRST 10 LEAGUE MATCHES AS WOOLWICH ARSENAL

	Date	Opponents	Result
1	2/9/1893	Newcastle United (h)	Drew 2–2
2	9/9/1893	Notts County (a)	Lost 3–2
3	11/9/1893	Walsall Town Swifts (h)	Won 4–0
4	25/9/1893	Grimsby Town (h)	Won 3–1
5	30/9/1893	Newcastle United (a)	Lost 6–0
6	21/10/1893	Small Heath (a)	Lost 4–1
7	28/10/1893	Liverpool (h)	Lost 5–0
8	11/11/1893	Ardwick (h)	Won 1–0
9	13/11/1893	Rotherham Town (h)	Won 3–0
10	18/11/1893	Burton Swifts (a)	Lost 6–2

	Date	Opponents	Result
1	4/4/1914	Bristol City (a)	Drew 1–1
2	10/4/1914	Stockport County (h)	Won 4–0
3	11/4/1914	Leeds County (a)	Drew 0–0
4	13/4/1914	Stockport County (h)	Won 4–0
5	18/4/1914	Clapton Orient (h)	Drew 2–2
6	23/4/1914	Grimsby Town (h)	Won 2–0
7	25/4/1914	Glossop (a)	Won 2–0
8	1/9/1914	Glossop (h)	Won 3–0
9	5/9/1914	Wolverhampton Wanderers (a)	Lost 0–1
10	8/9/1914	Glossop (a)	Won 4–0

LAST 10 LEAGUE MATCHES AT THE MANOR GROUND

	Date	Opponents	Result
1	26/4/1913	Middlesbrough	Drew 1–1
2	12/4/1913	Derby County	Lost 2–1
3	29/3/1913	Sheffield Wednesday	Lost 5–2
4	15/3/1913	West Bromwich Albion	Won 1–0
5	1/3/1913	Bradford City	Drew 1–1
6	8/2/1913	Oldham Athletic	Drew 0–0
7	18/1/1913	Sheffield United	Lost 3–1
8	28/12/1912	Liverpool	Drew 1–1
9	25/12/1912	Notts County	Drew 0–0
10	14/12/1912	Tottenham Hotspur	Lost 3–0

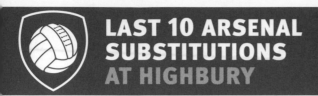
Player	Time
1= **Bergkamp for Reyes** v Wigan Athletic, 7/5/2006	79 minutes
= **Van Persie for Hleb** v Wigan Athletic, 7/5/2006	79 minutes
3 **Ljunberg for Pires** v Wigan Athletic, 7/5/2006	74 minutes
4= **Henry for Van Persie** v Tottenham Hotspur, 22/4/2006	62 minutes
= **Fabregas for Diaby** v Tottenham Hotspur, 22/4/2006	62 minutes
6 **Eboue for Senderos** v Tottenham Hotspur, 22/4/2006	54 minutes
7= **Bergkamp for Hleb** v Villarreal, 19/4/2006	80 minutes
= **Van Persie for Ljungberg** v Villarreal, 19/4/2006	80 minutes
9 **Bergkamp for Van Persie** v West Bromwich Albion, 15/4/2006	72 minutes
10 **Pires for Hleb** v West Bromwich Albion, 15/4/2006	71 minutes

FIRST 10 ARSENAL SUBSTITUTIONS AT THE EMIRATES

	Player	Time
1	**Van Persie for Adebayor** v Aston Villa, 19/8/2006	65 minutes
2	**Walcott for Ljungberg** v Aston Villa, 19/8/2006	73 minutes
3	**Flamini for Hoyte** v Aston Villa, 19/8/2006	80 minutes
4	**Henry for Adebayor** v Dinamo Zagreb, 23/8/2006	65 minutes
5	**Gilberto for Hleb** v Dinamo Zagreb, 23/8/2006	70 minutes
6	**Walcott for van Persie** v Dinamo Zagreb, 23/8/2006	81 minutes
7=	**Adebayor for Van Persie** v Middlesbrough 9/9/2006	69 minutes
=	**Baptista for Ljungberg** v Middlesbrough 9/9/2006	69 minutes
=	**Rosicky for Gilberto** v Middlesbrough, 9/9/2006	69 minutes
10	**Baptista for Hleb** v Manchester United, 17/9/2006	68 minutes

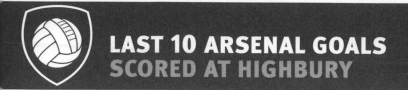

	Scorer	Time
1	**Thierry Henry (p)** v Wigan Athletic, 7/5/2006	76 minutes
2	**Thierry Henry** v Wigan Athletic, 7/5/2006	56 minutes
3	**Thierry Henry** v Wigan Athletic, 7/5/2006	35 minutes
4	**Robert Pires** v Wigan Athletic, 7/5/2006	8 minutes
5	**Thierry Henry** v Tottenham Hotspur, 22/4/2006	84 minutes
6	**Kolo Toure** v Villarreal, 19/4/2006	41 minutes
7	**Dennis Bergkamp** v West Bromwich Albion, 15/4/2006	89 minutes
8	**Robert Pires** v West Bromwich Albion, 15/4/2006	76 minutes
9	**Alexander Hleb** v West Bromwich Albion, 15/4/2006	44 minutes
10	**Abou Diaby** v Aston Villa, 1/4/2006	80 minutes

10 FIRST KISSES
OF ARSENAL FOLK*

1 **Manuel Almunia** 'My mum's, I guess.'

2 **Denilson** '9'

3 **Johan Djourou** '9 or 10'

4 **William Gallas** '10'

5 **Matt Lucas** 'A girl tried to kiss me when I was about 12.'

6 **Robin van Persie** '11'

7 **Robert Pires** '13'

8 **David Soul** 'In a game of spin-the-bottle when I was about 13.'

9 **Kolo Toure** 'When I met my wife.'

10 **Faye White** '8'

* To tie in with the Teenage Cancer Trust's run as Charity of the Season in 2008–09, the Arsenal programme asked a series of current and former players from the men's and ladies' sides, together with some celebrity fans, when their first kiss was.

10 BARGAIN-BASEMENT BUYS

	Player	Price
1	Eddie Hapgood (1927–44)	£950
2	Pat Jennings (1977–84)	£45,000
3	George Graham (1966–72)	£50,000
4	John Hollins (1979–82)	£75,000
5	Perry Groves (1986–92)	£75,000
6	Nigel Winterburn (1987–2000)	£350,000
7	Steve Bould (1988–98)	£390,000
8	Lee Dixon (1978–2001)	£400,000
9	Nicolas Anelka (1996–98)	£500,000
10	Patrick Vieira (1996–2004)	£3 million

10 GARY LEWIN
MILESTONES

1   **1980** Joins Arsenal as a 16-year old goalkeeper.

2   **1982** Signs for Barnet FC.

3   **1983** Trains in physiotherapy at London's Guy's Hospital.

4   **1984** Returns to the Club as reserve team physiotherapist.

5   **1986** Appointed first-team physiotherapist.

6   **1995** Appoints his cousin Colin Lewin to the Club physiotherapy team.

7   **1996** Appointed physiotherapist for England national team.

8   **2007** During the Carling Cup Final unblocks the airway of Chelsea skipper John Terry, possibly saving his life.

9   **2008** Credited with saving the career of Eduardo, after the striker's leg break at Birmingham City.

10   **2008** Appointed head of physiotherapy at the FA and leaves Arsenal after 1,205 matches as first-team physio.

10 BROKEN BONES

	Player	Break	Date
1	Joe Mercer	Broken leg	April 1954
2	Gordon Nutt	Cracked shin	September 1955
3	John Snedden	Broken ankle	December 1960
4	Jack McClelland	Broken collarbone	August 1963
5	David Jenkins	Broken leg	Summer 1965
6	Alan Ball	Broken leg	April 1974
7	Steve Morrow	Broken arm	April 1993
8	Ian Selley	Broken leg	February 1995
9	Rami Shaaban	Broken leg	December 2002
10	Eduardo	Broken leg	February 2008

TREATMENT TABLE

10 UNUSUAL INJURIES AND ILLNESSES

1   **Charlie George** The darling of the North Bank cut off his toe with a lawnmower.

2   **Perry Groves** The winger injured his head when he bashed it against the dugout roof while celebrating a goal.

3   **Thierry Henry** Hit himself in the face with the corner flag while celebrating a goal against Chelsea in May 2000.

4   **Andy Linighan** Was brave enough to continue in the 1993 FA Cup replay despite a broken nose. He even headed the winning goal!

5   **Steve Morrow** Broke his arm after falling off Tony Adams's shoulder while celebrating the 1993 League Cup Final victory.

6   **David Seaman** Broke a bone reaching for his television remote control.

7   **David Seaman** A second entry for the time he injured himself reeling in his catch while fishing.

8   **Alan Skirton** The 'Highbury Express' had his career derailed for 18 months by tuberculosis.

9   **Patrick Vieira** Injured his knees in 1997 while celebrating a goal against Manchester United with a slide across the Highbury turf.

10 **Richard Wright** After leaving the Gunners, the goalkeeper twisted his ankle while warming up for an Everton match.

1   **The Arsenal Charitable Trust** Formed in 1992, the trust distributes funds to local causes.

2   **Childline** This became the first 'Arsenal charity of the season' for the 2003–04 campaign.

3   **The David Rocastle Trust** Founded in 2005, it exists to assist David's family and support community projects and charities.

4   **Diambars Institute** Fronted by former Arsenal captain Patrick Vieira, this African initiative provides African children with education both on and off the pitch.

5   **The Kanu Heart Foundation** The striker Kanu, who once had a life-saving heart operation, fronts this charity for African children with heart conditions.

6   **Stand Up, Speak Out** Thierry Henry, who appeared on advertisements for UNICEF, set up this anti-racist initiative.

7   **Teenage Cancer Trust** The charity of the 2008–09 campaign, this is also backed by Who singer and Gunners fan Roger Daltrey.

8   **Treehouse** Arsenal's charity of the season for 2007–08, this was set up by parents (including Arsenal fan Nick Hornby) who have children diagnosed with autism.

9   **Willow Foundation** Set up by Bob Wilson and his wife, Megs, in memory of their daughter Anna, who died of cancer.

10 **Help a London Child** Emirates Stadium hosts numerous charity events, including a ball in aid of the children's charity in June 2009.

10 POPULAR
ARSENAL PUBS

1	**The Arsenal Tavern,** Blackstock Road, N4
2	**The Auld Triangle,** St Thomas Road, N4
3	**The Bank of Friendship,** Blackstock Road, N5
4	**The Canonbury Tavern,** Canonbury Place, N1
5	**The Famous Cock Tavern,** Upper Street, N1
6	**The Gunners,** Blackstock Road, N5
7	**The Hen and Chickens,** Highbury Corner, N1
8	**The Herbert Chapman,** Holloway Road, N7
9	**The Highbury Barn,** Highbury Park, N5
10	**The Worlds End,** Stroud Green Road, N4

10 FROM THE TRAINING-GROUND KITCHENS

1. **Banoffee pie** This was a favourite of Ray Parlour, Lauren and Freddie Ljungberg.

2. **Chilli sauce** When Rob the chef brought in some ultra-hot chilli sauce and youth-team player Rhema Obed bravely tried a whole spoonful, people had to stuff ice cubes into his mouth to cool him down.

3. **Key lime pie** Originating from Florida, this is often served prior to European away trips.

4. **Lasagne** The recipe for this was sent to the Club's chef by Tim De'ath, the head chef at West Ham United.

5. **Mulligatawny soup** This was a favourite of soup fan David Seaman, who also on FA Cup Final day always ordered two bowls of lobster bisque.

6. **Piri piri chicken** The Nandos restaurant is so popular among Arsenal players that Rob added this to the training-ground menu.

7. **Prawn risotto** This was cooked at the training ground by Theo Walcott.

8. **Soup** Manuel Almunia once asked Rob to teach him how to pass soup through a sieve.

9. **Southern fried chicken** When Rob introduced this to the lunch menu prior to away matches, the Gunners lost two games on the trot – against Stoke City and Manchester City it was promptly removed.

10. **Tandoori salmon** This is a popular dish among the first-year scholars at Arsenal.

10 FOR TEA*

1   Jeremie Aliadiere

2   Emmanuel Eboue

3   Mathieu Flamini

4   Alexander Hleb

5   Jermaine Pennant

6   Phillppe Senderos

7   Ryan Smith

8   Patrick Vieira

9   Moritz Volz

10   Theo Walcott

* When interviewed during their Arsenal player days by the *Official Arsenal Magazine*, players were asked whether they preferred tea or coffee.

10 CRICKETING GUNNERS

	Player	County or country
1	Brian Close	Yorkshire, Somerset and England
2	Denis Compton	Middlesex and England
3	George Cox	Sussex
4	Ted Drake	Hampshire
5	Andy Ducat	Surrey and England
6	Ian Gould	Middlesex and Sussex
7	Jimmy Gray	Hampshire
8	Wally Hardinge	Kent and England
9	Arthur Milton	Gloucestershire and England
10	Harry Murrell	Kent and Middlesex

1   **Dave Bacuzzi**   Son of Joe Bacuzzi, who played for Fulham.

2   **Mel Charles**   Brother of Welsh star John Charles.

3   **George Eastham**   Son of George Eastham Sr, who played in the Northern Irish League.

4   **Alexander Hleb**   Brother of Belarusian international Vyacheslav.

8   **Pat Jennings**   Father of Pat Jennings Jnr who has played in goal for Derry City and Sligo Rovers.

5   **Nwankwo Kanu**   Brother of Chris Kanu, who played for Peterborough United.

6   **Andy Linighan**   Brother of David and Brian Linighan, who played for Ipswich Town and Sheffield Wednesday.

7   **John Lukic**   Father of John Lukic, who played for various clubs, including Nottingham Forest.

9   **Christopher Wreh**   Cousin of Liberia and AC Milan legend George Weah.

10   **Ian Wright**   Stepfather of Manchester City's Shaun Wright-Phillips and father of Southampton's Bradley Wright-Phillips.

TOP 10 BRITISH COUNTIES WHERE PLAYERS WERE BORN*

	County	Players
1	London	58
2	Lanarkshire	15
3	Yorkshire	14
4	Lancashire	13
5	Essex	12
6	Durham	11
7	Surrey	9
8	Kent	6
9	Glamorgan	5
10	Suffolk	4

* Covers players who have appeared in at least one Arsenal match since World War II.

THE 10 HIGHEST-SCORING ENGLAND GAMES
AT HIGHBURY

	Match and score	Date
1=	England 7–1 Spain	9/12/1931
=	England 6–2 Hungary	2/12/1936
3	England 6–1 Belgium	19/3/1923
4=	England 4–2 Sweden	19/11/1947
=	England 6–0 Switzerland	1/12/1948
6=	England 3–2 Italy	14/11/1934
=	England 4–1 Luxembourg	28/9/1961
8=	England 2–2 Yugoslavia	22/11/1950
=	England 2–2 France	3/10/1951
10=	England 3–0 Europe XI	26/10/1938
=	England 3–0 France	3/5/1947

TOP 10 IRISH/NORTHERN IRISH GUNNERS

	Player	Appearances
1	David O'Leary	719
2	Pat Rice	527
3	Pat Jennings	338
4	Sammy Nelson	326
5	Frank Stapleton	306
6	Liam Brady	299
7	Joe Haverty	122
8	John Devine	111
9	Niall Quinn	81
10	Steve Morrow	85

10 NORTHERN GUNNERS

	Player	Born
1	George Armstrong	Hebburn, County Durham
2	Alan Ball	Farnworth, Lancashire
3	Lee Dixon	Manchester
4	George Eastham	Blackpool, Lancashire
5	David Jack	Bolton, Lancashire
6	Bob McNab	Huddersfield, Yorkshire
7	John Radford	Hemsworth, Yorkshire
8	Graham Rix	Doncaster, Yorkshire
9	David Seaman	Rotherham, Yorkshire
10	Alan Sunderland	Mexborough, Yorkshire

10 ISLINGTON GUNNERS

	Player	Played
1	David Bacuzzi	1960–63
2	Jay Bothroyd	2000
3	Mark Flatts	1992–94
4	Charlie George	1969–74
5	John Halls	2001–04
6	Raphael Meade	1981–84
7	Eddie McGoldrick	1993–95
8	Ryan Smith	2003–06
9	Paolo Vernazza	1997–2000
10	Chris Whyte	1981–85

10 EAST LONDON
GUNNERS

	Player	Born
1	Tony Adams	Romford
2	Sol Campbell	Newham
3	Danny Clapton	Stepney
4	Ashley Cole	Stepney
5	Perry Groves	Bow
6	Vic Groves	Stepney
7	George Male	West Ham
8	David O'Leary	Stoke Newington
9	Ray Parlour	Romford
10	Richie Powling	Barking

10 SCOTTISH GUNNERS

	Player	**Played**
1	Billy Blyth	1914–29
2	James Charteris	1888–90
3	Gavin Crawford	1891–98
4	Alex Forbes	1948–56
5	George Graham	1966–72
6	Frank Hill	1932–36
7	Alex James	1929–37
8	Jimmy Logie	1939–55
9	Frank McLintock	1964–73
10	Charlie Nicholas	1983–88

10 CUP REPLAY SAGAS

1 **v Rotherham United, FA Cup, 1959–60** This third-round tie ended 2–2 at Rotherham, then 1–1 at Highbury. The replay at Sheffield Wednesday saw Rotherham win a u

2 **v Gillingham, League Cup, 1966–67** Two successive 1–1 draws led to a second replay, in which Arsenal triumphed 5–0.

3 **v Derby County FA Cup, 1971–72** Having drawn 2–2 and 0–0 in this fifth-round tie, a Ray Kennedy goal was enough to make it third time lucky.

4 **v Blackpool, League Cup, 1976–77** A 2–0 win saw Arsenal through to the fourth round after two attempts had ended 1–1 and 0–0.

5 **v Sheffield Wednesday, FA Cup 1978–79** An epic run of five matches was needed to separate the Gunners and the Owls.

6 **v Liverpool, FA Cup 1979–80** A Brian Talbot header eventually won the semi-final for Arsenal, but not before the first three matches had ended all square.

7 **v Leeds United, FA Cup 1982–83** Following a brace of 1–1 draws, the Gunners sailed through to the fifth round 2–1.

8 **v Luton Town, FA Cup 1985–86** After drawing 2–2 at Luton, the Highbury replay ended 0–0, so it was back to Kenilworth Road, where the Gunners lost 3–0.

9 **v Liverpool, League Cup 1988–89** The Merseysiders won the third instalment of this third-round tie 2–1 at Anfield.

10 **v Leeds United, FA Cup 1990–91** After three draws, the Gunners finally prevailed 2–1 at Elland Road in this fourth-round tie.

10 ACADEMY GRADUATES

	Player	Moved to
1	Jeremie Aliadiere	Middlesbrough
2	David Bentley	Tottenham Hotspur
3	Ashley Cole	Chelsea
4	Sebastian Larsson	Birmingham City
5	Fabrice Muamba	Bolton Wanderers
6	Jermaine Pennant	Liverpool
7	Steven Sidwell	Reading
8	Anthony Stokes	Sunderland
9	Stuart Taylor	Aston Villa
10	Moritz Volz	Fulham

10 NOTABLE CAPTAINS*

1   **Tom Parker, 1926–33** The first trophy-winning skipper, he led the Club to the 1930 FA Cup Final and the first League title.

2   **Eddie Hapgood, 1927–44** Won five titles with the Club, including one as captain in 1937–38.

3   **Joe Mercer, 1946–55** Having led the Gunners to the 1950 FA Cup Final and the 1953 title, he insisted that captaining Arsenal was the greatest honour in sport.

4   **Frank McLintock, 1964–73** Skipper of the Fairs Cup and Double-winning teams.

5   **Pat Rice, 1967–80** Led Arsenal to three FA Cup Finals, including the victory over Manchester United in 1979.

6   **Kenny Sansom, 1980–88** Nobody won more England caps as an Arsenal captain than Sansom, who wore the armband as the Club won the 1987 League Cup.

7   **Tony Adams, 1983–2002** He became the Club's youngest captain in January 1988 at the age of 21, lifting four titles, two League Cups, three FA Cups and a European Cup Winners' Cup.

8   **Patrick Vieira 1996–2005** Won two FA Cups and a League title during his captaincy, along with the 49-match unbeaten run.

9   **Thierry Henry, 1999–2007** Led Arsenal to its first UEFA Champions League Final and in its first campaign at Emirates Stadium.

10   **Cesc Fabregas, 2003–** The first Spanish captain of the Club.

* Dates refer to each players' entire Arsenal career, not just their spell as captain.

THE 10 MOST-REFERENCED PLAYERS IN *ARSENAL STADIUM HISTORY*

	Player	References
1	Thierry Henry	33
2	Dennis Bergkamp	32
3	Cliff Bastin	28
4	George Graham	27
5	Patrick Vieira	26
6	Tony Adams	25
7	David Seaman	21
8	Robert Pires	18
9	Leslie Compton	17
10	Charlie George	16

10 WORLD WAR II
GUEST PLAYERS*

	Player	Club
1	Joe Bacuzzi	Fulham
2	Len Goulden	West Ham United
3	Bill Griffiths	Cardiff City
4	Reg Halton	Bury
5	Stanley Matthews	Stoke City
6	Stan Mortensen	Blackpool
7	Ronnie Rooke	Fulham
8	Bill Shankly	Preston North End
9	Joe Wilson	Brighton and Hove Albion
10	Bill Wrigglesworth	Manchester United

* Guest players were essentially loan players during wartime.

10 UNSUNG HEROES

1   Ian Allinson
He was a spectacular 'super-sub' during the 1980s, often rising from the bench to change a game, including against Tottenham Hotspur in the FA Cup.

2   Alf Baker
During his 11 years at Arsenal 'Doughy' played in every position on the pitch.

3   Denilson
He has been identified as an unsung hero by no less an authority than Arsène Wenger, who said, 'He does not attract too much limelight because he is discreet, does not talk and does his job.'

4   Gilles Grimandi
He was a dependable, adaptable option for five years, during which time the Club won two Doubles. Grimandi now scouts for Arsenal.

5   Perry Groves
He might have faced a degree of mockery but he left the Club with two League Championship medals in his back pocket.

6   Andy Linighan
He once joked that he thought his first name was 'Boo', referring to the reaction of some when his name was read out on the team-sheet. He scored the winner in the FA Cup Final against Sheffield Wednesday in 1993.

7   **Oleg Luzhny**

He was a loyal and dependable squad member, happy to appear in a variety of positions when called upon. He excelled in the Double-winning campaign of 2001–02.

8   **Brian Marwood**

He was instrumental in the Club's title-winning campaign of 1988–89, setting up numerous goals for Alan Smith.

9   **Bruce Rioch**

At the helm for just one – trophyless – season, Rioch was nonetheless a useful bridge between the George Graham and Arsène Wenger eras. He was in charge when Dennis Bergkamp signed for the Club.

10   **Ronnie Rooke**

Rarely mentioned among the Club's greatest names, he scored 68 goals in 88 matches for Arsenal – an astonishing strike rate. He also scored in the FA Cup.

10 RUNNERS-UP

	Competition	Date	Losing to
1	FA Cup	1927	Cardiff City
2	FA Cup	1932	Newcastle United
3	FA Cup	1952	Newcastle United
4	FA Cup	1972	Leeds United
5	Division One	1973	Liverpool
6	FA Cup	1978	Ipswich Town
7	FA Cup	1980	West Ham United
8	Premiership	1999	Manchester United
9	Premiership	2000	Manchester United
10	FA Cup	2001	Liverpool

10 GUNNERS WHO PASSED AWAY YOUNG

1   Bob Benson aged 33, 1916
2   Alexander Cale aged 33, 1914
3   Tommy Caton aged 30, 1993
4   Herbert Chapman aged 56, 1934
5   Niccolo Galli aged 17, 1999
6   Alex James aged 51, 1953
7   Sidney Pugh aged 24, 1944
8   David Rocastle aged 33, 2001
9   Paul Vaessen aged 39, 2001
10 Tom Whittaker aged 58, 1956

	Goals	Season
1	17	1998–99
2	18	1990–91
3	28	1993–94
4=	32	1995–96
=	32	1996–97
6	33	1997–98
7	36	1988–89
8=	38	1989–90
=	38	1992–93
10	46	1991–92

* The years in which Bould, Winterburn, Dixon and Adams played together for the Club.

10 PLAYERS BORN ON THE 10TH OF THE MONTH

	Player	Birthday
1	Tony Adams	10/10/1966
2	Tommy Baldwin	10/6/1945
3	Paul Davies	10/10/1952
4	Charlie George	10/10/1950
5	Cyril Grant	10/7/1920
6	Peter Nicholas	10/11/1959
7	Kevin O'Flanagan	10/6/1919
8	Jimmy Rimmer	10/2/1948
9	Sylvain Wiltord	10/5/1974
10	John Woodward	10/1/1949

10 AWKWARD OPPONENTS

1 **Nicolas Anelka**
Since leaving Arsenal he has scored three times against the Club in the colours of Manchester City and three times for Bolton Wanderers, two of them coming in a frustrating 3–1 defeat at the Reebok in 2006.

2 **Bolton Wanderers**
Then of the old First Division, Bolton knocked Arsenal out of the 1994 FA Cup after a shock 3–1 victory at Highbury. During Arsène Wenger's reign, they have often frustrated the Gunners. In the first ever meeting between the two sides in 1895, Bolton knocked Arsenal out of the FA Cup.

3 **Brentford**
The west Londoners have won five of their ten League matches against Arsenal, the best percentage record of any London club.

4 **Former Spurs players**
Arsenal have lost two successive European Cup Finals thanks to goals from former Tottenham stars. First, Nayim's famous chip meant the Gunners lost the 1995 European Cup Winners' Cup Final. Then, in 2000, the former Spurs man Gheorghe Popescu hit the decisive spot-kick to deny Arsenal the UEFA Cup.

5 **Robbie Fowler**
Scored hat-tricks against Arsenal in successive seasons, the first of which (in 1994) was the fastest ever Premiership hat-trick, just to rub salt in the wound.

6 Jimmy Floyd Hasselbaink
Scored against Arsenal for Leeds United twice in the 1997–98 season and twice in the following campaign, including the goal that effectively ended the Club's Premiership challenge. He then scored twice against the Gunners for Chelsea and once for Middlesbrough.

7 Liverpool
Having won the League Championship at Anfield in 1989, the Gunners then won only two of their next 14 League clashes there.

8 Wayne Rooney
In his first four seasons in senior football Rooney scored against Arsenal four times. The first of these, in October 2002, ended a 24-match unbeaten run. Then, in 2004, his strike brought to an end an unbeaten run that had stretched for 49 games.

9 Teddy Sheringham
The England striker has netted against the Gunners for four different clubs: Nottingham Forest, Manchester United, Tottenham Hotspur and Portsmouth.

10 Valencia
The Gunners have been sent crashing out of European competitions three times by the Spaniards. The most painful was when they beat Arsenal on penalties in the 1980 European Cup Winners' Cup Final.

10 FORMER GUNNERS' GOALS AGAINST ARSENAL

	Player	Match	Date
1	Jeremie Aliadiere	v Middlesbrough	13/12/2008
2	Nicolas Anelka	v Manchester City	10/9/2002
3	Nicolas Anelka	v Bolton Wanderers	25/11/2006
4	Kevin Campbell	v Nottingham Forest	29/8/1995
5	Kevin Campbell	v Everton	21/4/2001
6	Lee Chapman	v Leeds United	25/1/1993
7	Paul Merson	v Aston Villa	9/12/2001
8	Andy Cole	v Manchester United	19/2/1997
9	Niall Quinn	v Sunderland	15/1/2000
10	Emmanuel Petit	v Chelsea	1/1/2003

TOP 10 SELLING ISSUES OF *THE GOONER* FANZINE*

1   **Issue 88 (August 1998)** There was only one word to sum up Wenger's first full season in charge – *magnifique!*

2   **Issue 100 (December 1999)** *The Gooner* celebrates its century with a look back over the 12 years since issue 1 hit the street.

3   **Issue 107 (December 2000)** Our first glimpse of what the new stadium at Ashburton Grove was going to look like and it's fair to say we were impressed!

4   **Issue 115 (October 2001)** Fans were asking whether the defensive guard of Seaman and Adams were on the way out as Richard Wright and Matthew Upson excelled.

5   **Issue 129 (November 2002)** Record goal-scorer Thierry Henry celebrates that goal "from the halfway line" against Spurs.

6   **Issue 146 (May 2004)** The picture on the cover may have only contained an inflatable trophy but we'd just won the League at White Hart Lane...again!

7   **Issue 150 (October 2004)** The incredible unbeaten run had just come to an end, so this was the time to "Hail the 49ers".

8   **Issue 165 (May 2006)** The end of the last season at Highbury and the cover needs nothing more than a picture of the East Stand.

9   **Issue 171 (December 2006)** The goalscoring form of Emmanuel "The main Manu" Adebayor is celebrated as Henry is rested.

10 **Issue 178 (September 2007)** Arsène Wenger signs a new contract much to the relief of the fans.

* Compiled by Mike Francis, editor of *The Gooner*.

10 TOUGH DEFEATS

1   Arsenal 0–1 Ipswich, FA Cup Final, 6/5/1978
Roger Osborne netted the winner at Wembley, prompting tears from
one David O'Leary and several thousand Arsenal fans. A year on, the
Gunners were back and won the Final.

2   Arsenal 2–3 Luton Town, Littlewoods Cup Final, 24/4/1988
After an exciting, seesaw tie it was Mark Stein who grabbed the
winner with less than a minute on the clock. He thus denied
the Gunners the chance for a second successive victory in
the competition.

**3   Arsenal 1–3 Tottenham Hotspur, FA Cup semi-final,
14/4/1991**
Few Gunners can forget the day when goals from Paul Gascoigne and
Gary Lineker denied Arsenal a place in the Final. All wish they could.

**4   Arsenal 1–2 Real Zaragoza, European Cup Winners' Cup
Final, 10/5/1995**
The Gunners were minutes from a penalty shoot-out in the Final,
with spot-kick expert David Seaman in goal. Then former Tottenham
man Nayim scored the winner from the halfway line.

**5   Arsenal 1–2 Manchester United, FA Cup semi-final replay,
14/4/1999**
Peter Schmeichel saved a Dennis Bergkamp penalty, then Ryan
Giggs scored a dramatic winner after running from the halfway line.

6 **Arsenal 0–0 Galatasaray (Galatasaray won on penalties), UEFA Cup Final, 17/5/2000**
After a match of missed chances, the game went to a shoot-out. Davor Suker and Patrick Vieira missed their spot-kicks, while former Tottenham defender Gheorghe Popescu hit the winner for Galatasaray.

7 **Manchester United 6–1 Arsenal, Premiership, 24/2/2001**
A Dwight Yorke hat-trick completed in just 20 first-half minutes was a low point on a low day for the Gunners. A makeshift Arsenal defence struggled against on-form United and the scoreline showed it.

8 **Arsenal 1–2 Liverpool, FA Cup Final, 12/5/2001**
The Gunners dominated the game but found it hard to score until Freddie Ljungberg got the apparent winner on 70 minutes. Then Michael Owen scored twice in the final eight minutes.

9 **Arsenal 1–2 Chelsea, Champions League quarter-final, second leg, 6/4/2004**
After Arsenal had taken the lead through Jose Antonio Reyes, a Jens Lehmann error gifted Frank Lampard an equalizer. Then, with three minutes left, Wayne Bridge stunned Highbury with the winner.

10 **Tottenham Hotspur 5–1 Arsenal, Carling Cup semi-final, 22/1/2008**
Prior to this game, Spurs had not beaten Arsenal for nine years. Emmanuel Adebayor's 70th-minute strike was the only consolation as Spurs ran riot against a young Gunners team.

1   **1946** Begins working at the Club as a part-time errand boy at the tender age of 11.

2   **1950** Takes his first full-time position, as an office junior in the box office.

3   **1954** Transferred to the accounts team.

4   **1965** Promoted to Assistant Club Secretary.

5   **1973** Replaces Bob Wall as Club Secretary (Wall becaming General Manager).

6   **1983** Becomes Managing Director and is appointed to the board.

7   **2000** Awarded an OBE for his services to football in the Queen's Birthday Honours List. The same year he retired as Managing Director to mastermind the Club's relocation to the Emirates Stadium.

8   **2004** Awarded the freedom of the London Borough of Islington.

9   **2007** Transfers 147 shares in the Club to chairman Peter Hill-Wood.

10 **2008** Is named Acting Managing Director after the departure of Keith Edelman.

10 GREAT GOALS
AGAINST ARSENAL

1   **Alan Clarke for Leeds United, May 1972** After a sweeping move downfield, Clarke headed home from distance at Wembley.

2   **Keith Birchin for Birmingham City, October 1977** From a seemingly impossibe angle, Birchin somehow managed to score and – subsequently – win Goal of the Season on ITV's *The Big Match*.

3   **Paul Gascoigne for Tottenham Hotspur, April 1991** 'Is he going to have a crack? He is, you know!'

4   **Nayim for Real Zaragoza, May 1995** Lobbing David Seaman from the halfway line to win the European Cup Winners' Cup, this goal was as brilliant as it was painful.

5   **Ryan Giggs for Manchester United, April 1999** Running half the length of the pitch and weaving through the defence, Giggs volleyed past David Seaman to send United to the Final.

6   **Gabriel Batistuta for Fiorentina, October 1999** The Argentinian shot from a tight angle across David Seaman and into the roof of the net, knocking the Gunners out of the Champions League.

7   **Wayne Rooney for Everton, October 2002** He smashed the ball home to end Arsenal's 30-match unbeaten run.

8   **Michael Essien for Chelsea, December 2006** Essien cracked the ball from a distance and it soared into the top of Lehmann's net.

9   **Geovanni for Hull City, September 2008** He danced past a challenge on the left and moved infield, whereupon he smashed a sensational right-foot shot into the top left corner of the net.

10 **David Bentley for Tottenham Hotspur, October 2008** The former Gunner chipped Almunia in this North London derby.

THE 10 HIGHEST VICTORIES IN THE RACING CLUB DE PARIS FIXTURE*

	Match and score	Year
1	Racing Club 2–7 Arsenal	1930
2=	Racing Club 0–5 Arsenal	1938
=	Racing Club 0–5 Arsenal	1951
4	Racing Club 1–5 Arsenal	1950
5	Arsenal 4–0 Racing Club	1953
6	Racing Club 2–5 Arsenal	1932
7	Racing Club 1–4 Arsenal	1961
8=	Racing Club 0–3 Arsenal	1934
=	Racing Club 0–3 Arsenal	1962
10=	Racing Club 2–4 Arsenal	1953
=	Racing Club 1–3 Arsenal	1954
=	Racing Club 0–2 Arsenal	1937

* Source: *The Official Arsenal Miscellany*.

10 GUNNERS WHO RETURNED TO WORK
BEHIND THE SCENES

	Player	Position
1	Steve Bould	Head Coach of Under-18 Academy Side
2	Liam Brady	Head of Youth Development
3	David Court	Assistant Head of Youth Development
4	Paul Davis	Youth Team Coach
5	Steve Gatting	Youth Team Coach
6	Charlie George	Arsenal Legends Tour Guide
7	Gilles Grimandi	Scout
8	Steve Morrow	International Partnerships Performance Supervisor
9	Pat Rice	Assistant Manager
10	Kenny Sansom	Arsenal Legends Tour Guide

10 MEMORABLE '1–0 TO THE ARSENAL' VICTORIES

	Match and score	Competition	Date
1	Arsenal 1–0 Hull City	FA Cup semi-final	March 1930
2	Juventus 0–1 Arsenal	European Cup Winners' Cup Final	April 1980
3	Liverpool 0–1 Arsenal	Division One	March 1991
4	Arsenal 1–0 Tottenham Hotspur	FA Cup semi-final	April 1993
5	Arsenal 1–0 Paris St Germain	European Cup Winners' Cup semi-final, second leg	April 1994
6	Arsenal 1–0 Parma	European Cup Winners' Cup Final	May 1994
7	Arsenal 1–0 Manchester United	Premiership	March 1998
8	Arsenal 1–0 Manchester United	Premiership	May 2002
9	Arsenal 1–0 Southampton	FA Cup Final	May 2003
10	Arsenal 1–0 Villarreal	UEFA Champions League semi-final	April 2006

10 DISASTROUS DEBUTS

1   **Sidney Pugh v Birmingham City (a), April 1939** Pugh suffered a kidney injury in the opening minutes and never played for the Club again.

2   **Jack Kelsey v Charlton Athletic (h), February 1951** The goalkeeper conceded five in his opening match, which ended 5-2.

3   **Peter Simpson v Chelsea (h), March 1964** Simpson was marking Bobby Tambling, who scored four goals in this 4-2 defeat.

4   **Tony Adams v Sunderland (h), November 1973** Adams put his shorts on back to front, gave the ball away for the visitors' opener and had a goal disallowed.

5   **Willie Young v Ipswich (h), March 1977** After a torrid afternoon, Young was booed by the fans, who told him to 'go back to Spurs'.

6   **Lee Chapman v Stoke City, August 1982** Chapman had a poor start against the team that sold him to Arsenal, as the Gunners lost 2-1.

7   **John Jensen v Norwich City, August 1992** Jensen was not solely responsible for the 4-2 loss, but it wasn't a great start for him, or for the Club in its debut Premiership tie.

8   **Jason Crowe v Birmingham City (h), October 1997** Crowe came on as a sub and was sent off 33 seconds later for a high tackle.

9   **Edu v Middlesbrough, April 2001** On his home debut Edu scored an own goal as the Gunners lost 3-0, effectively handing the Premiership title to Manchester United.

10   **Jose Antonio Reyes v Middlesbrough, February 2004** On his first full start, Reyes sliced the ball into his own net.

10 DELIGHTFUL DEBUTS

1 **Jack Crayston v Liverpool (h), September 1934**
As the Gunners thrashed Liverpool 8–1, new boy Crayston scored one of the goals and set up another.

2 **Alf Kirchen v Tottenham Hotspur (a), March 1935**
As Arsenal thrashed their rivals 6–0, the debutant scored twice and set up Ted Drake for the fourth.

3 **Peter Marinello v Manchester United (a), January 1970**
The Scot dribbled fully 45 metres (50 yards), danced round goalkeeper Alex Stepney and slotted home.

4 **Wilf Rostron v Newcastle United (h), March 1975**
Sunderland-born Rostron scored against Newcastle United on his home debut and followed up with a goal in his second match four days later against Burnley.

5 **Gus Caesar v Manchester United (a), December 1985**
Lining up at right back, Caesar marked Jesper Olsen out of the game.

6 **Ian Wright v Southampton (a), September 1991**
Having scored in his debut against Leicester City in the League Cup, Wright smashed a hat-trick in this, his first League start for the Club.

7   Glenn Helder v Nottingham Forest (h), February 1995
The Dutchman was sensational in his first Arsenal appearance,
wowing the crowd with a combination of step-overs and willer tricks.

8   Freddie Ljungberg v Manchester United (h), September 1998
Defending Champions Man Utd were already two goals to the good
when the Swede came off the bench and beautifully chipped the ball
over Peter Schmeichel.

9   Jermaine Pennant v Southampton (h), May 2003
The game that began the 49-match unbeaten run was also notable
for a hat-trick from Pennant that contributed to a fine 6–1 victory.

10   Samir Nasri v West Bromwich Albion (h), August 2008
The French youngster scored in the fourth minute of this, his first
game for Arsenal. It turned out to be the winning goal.

10 OWN GOALS

1   Dan Lewis v Cardiff City, 23/4/1927
Goalkeeper Lewis initially saved a shot from Hugh Ferguson, but the
ball slipped from his grasp and his elbow accidentally sent it over
the goal line. This goal was enough to win the FA Cup for Cardiff City.

2   Dennis Evans v Blackpool, 17/12/1955
Believing he had heard the final whistle, the Merseysider smashed
the ball past his own goalkeeper, Con Sullivan, in celebration.
However, the whistle had come from the crowd and the goal stood.

3   George Graham v Ajax, 22/3/1972
In this European Cup quarter-final, second leg, Graham sent
the Gunners crashing out of the competition after heading past
Bob Wilson.

4   Tony Adams v Manchester United, 2/4/1989
As the run-in gathered pace, the captain was the hero when he put
the Gunners ahead at Old Trafford. However, just seven minutes later
he inadvertently converted Clayton Blackmore's cross.

5   David O'Leary v Sunderland, 5/1/1991
This strike was not unlike Lee Dixon's against Coventry City.
Fortunately, goals from Alan Smith and Anders Limpar were enough
to seal victory.

6   Lee Dixon v Coventry City, 7/9/1991
The defender lobbed the ball over the head of David Seaman from
28 metres (30 yards). This led to a 2–1 defeat, the Gunners' first at
home in the League for 18 months.

7 **Silvinho v Middlesbrough, 14/4/2001**
Just four minutes earlier, Brazilian Edu had scored an own goal. Then his compatriot and team-mate Silvinho also had a red face when he sliced the ball past David Seaman.

8 **Kolo Toure v Aston Villa, 5/4/2003**
In the 70th minute, the Ivorian accidentally netted past Arsenal goalkeeper Stuart Taylor, cancelling out team-mate Freddie Ljungberg's opener.

9 **Lauren v Manchester City, 31/8/2003**
In the 11th minute there appeared to be little danger as Lauren dealt with a routine long pass. However, he accidentally shinned the ball past an appalled Jens Lehmann.

10 **Julio Baptista v Tottenham Hotspur, 24/1/2007**
The Brazilian accidentally put Spurs 2–0 ahead with an own goal but turned hero when his two goals at the correct end left the first leg of this League Cup semi-final level.

ACKNOWLEDGEMENTS

The author is extremely grateful for the assistance of Nick Payman, Christopher Bevan, Samir Singh, Trevor Davies, Rob Kemp, Steve Bould, Dennis Bergkamp, Daniel Granditer, Paul Kaye, Tom Watt, Shez Shafiq, Damian Schogger, Ashley Perry, Lucian Randall, Andy Exley, Chris Morris, Matt Weiner, Ruth Wiseall, Aron Lazarus, Hardeep Singh Kohli, Shovell, Robert Peston, Chris Hollins, Kenny Sansom, Bob Wilson, Jenny Davies, Jonathan Sacerdoti and Rita Wright.

The publisher would like to thank Fred Ollier and Rab MacWilliam for their help with fact-checking the book.

Executive Editor Trevor Davies
Editor Ruth Wiseall
Design Manager Tokiko Morishima
Illustrator Willie Ryan
Production Manager David Hearn